YOUR SOUL IS CALLING

UNLEARN THE CRAP

—— AND ——

LEVEL UP

FOREWORD BY LORAL LANGEMEIER | THE MILLIONAIRE MAKER

KATHY BALDWIN

AWARD-WINNING AUTHOR

ISBN: 978-1-966798-15-6

"Our deepest fear is not that we are inadequate.
Our deepest fear is that we are powerful beyond all measure.
It is our *light* — not our darkness that most frightens us."
—Marianne Williamson

Table of Contents

Dedication

This book is dedicated to Rick,

As I look back on our journey together, through our rollercoaster of highs and lows, I am filled with heartfelt emotions. It has been a blessing to have you in my life. With you, I have loved and been loved; I have walked with you, cried with you, and been challenged by and with you. Together we have been through more of life's obstacles than many couples ever go through in their entire lifetimes.

As we began our journey together, we carried the weight of our pasts, oblivious to the challenges ahead of us. During the course of our story, both of us were pushed to the brink of our capacity in unexpected ways.

While our journey was tumultuous, the lessons we learned were transformational. It was you who held me up in my darkest hour. In the face of adversity, you stood beside me and became my hero. Because of you, I carry the lessons we learned along the way in my heart, as a reminder that I can face anything with courage and grace.

Words cannot capture the depth of my gratitude for the support you gave me. Your presence, compassion, and unwavering belief in me helped pave the way for my healing and recovery. Without you, I wouldn't have found the strength to RiseUP from the ashes and rebuild my life. Without you, this book would not be possible.

As I release my inner convictions about personal success and empowerment out into the world, I cannot overlook the profound impact you've had on my transformation. Our shared experiences, however challenging, have ultimately shaped who I am today.

May this dedication serve as a testament to the strength and love we gained from the ruins of the past. It is a tribute to our resilience, and the support we offered one another.

Your unwavering presence and support have left an undeniable mark on my life.

From the depths of my heart and soul, I am grateful, thankful, and blessed you are in my life.

Kathy

Foreword

After dedicating most of my life to helping people from all walks of life become millionaires, I've come to realize an undeniable truth. Without your health and good sense of self – money is meaningless. That may sound a bit harsh, but if you think on it for a bit the reality is truly indisputable.

If you are sick or in pain, sleeping on silk sheets really doesn't make you feel better. Or if you suffer from an inferiority complex that tricks you into believing that your money is undeserved – causing you to not enjoy it or even save it – it is quite worthless.

That's why you must read *Unlearn the Crap about Personal Success & Empowerment*. This book peels back the layers that society has piled on you for decades. In it Kathy Baldwin make it clear that so much of your life is lived within the confines of collective truths that may or may not be your own personal beliefs. Then they do something that borders on magical. They actually show you how to reach your own personal conclusions so you can reach the success that you desire.

One of my favorite quotes in the book is, "Remember your power is in choice and decision. Power doesn't mean easy or fast, but it is your POWER to create." This quote is from chapter seven, which also contains an exercise to help you get clear on exactly who you are and what you want.

Another thing that impressed me about this book is the author's openness to her own obstacles in life. Her vulnerability and honesty throughout these pages really helps you to connect to the content, and gives confidence that if Kathy can overcome using these techniques, then so can you.

The entire book is filled with quotes, exercises, and information to help you RiseUP from wherever you are and take back your power. Once you understand who you are and what you want, creating and receiving money is a whole lot easier and much more fun.

I recommend you do exactly as Kathy says and *Unlearn the Crap* so you can earn and enjoy your money the way it was meant to be. You'll find *Personal Success and Empowerment* waiting on the other side.

Loral Langemeier
The Millionaire Maker

CHAPTER 1

Unveiling the Journey:
From Society's Blueprint to
Self-Discovery

My journey of self-discovery began at the tender age of twenty-one, on the day I became a parent. As I held this brand-new, little life in my arms, I had an overpowering and burning desire to create a better life for him. I had dreams of giving him everything good in the world. Unconditional love, safety and security. But I also wanted to give him even more than that. I wanted him to grow up with a strong sense of self-worth and belief in his own abilities. I wanted him to be able to know and understand his strengths and also be able to face challenges with courage and determination.

Because of my naive choices it was just the two of us. I had no other support whatsoever. In a way it seemed easier this way and in that moment of space and time, my perspective expanded. For the first time in my life I could see beyond my immediate surroundings. It was the beginning of a new comprehension of the beauty and complexity in the world. I saw possibilities not only for my new little boy but for myself as well. I began to feel a deeper meaning to life than I had ever known before. It was a profound moment of insight and revelation that had a lasting impact on my consciousness.

But there was one problem; I was caught in the web of societal expectations with which many of us are quite familiar. The well-trodden path of education. The need for job security. Only getting what you want through hard work. However, this maze of deception led me to a surprising and pivotal turning point – propelling me towards a profound pilgrimage of personal growth and self-discovery.

At first I embraced society's blueprint that had already been laid out before me. I recognized the importance of education as the foundation for success, so I pursued a higher education. Because I was a single parent, I made the brave decision to sign up for government assistance in order to provide a stable life for my son. This way I could ensure all of our basic needs were being met while I pursued the task of obtaining a degree in Business Administration, Sales, and Marketing Management. It was a very delicate balancing act that required sacrifices, sleepless nights, and uncompromising commitment. Not to mention the incredible resilience needed on a regular basis.

Being a single mom presented an abundant amount of challenges: the stress of financial burdens, the pressure to excel academically, and the constant need to provide for my child. These duties threatened me with an overwhelming feeling of responsibility and obligation. Yet, among these trials and tribulations I discovered a mysterious inner strength I never knew existed. It was within those very challenges that the seeds of self-discovery were sown.

I didn't know it at the time, but I would later learn that within every problem lies the seed to success. It was as if a small crack of light was being cast upon the darkness of my understanding. I started seeing the value in every experience as I began approaching challenges with an open mind and embracing them as gateways to discovery.

In the blind pursuit of self-improvement, resourcefulness became my greatest ally. Every waking moment was dedicated to carving out a better future for my son and myself. I took on the demanding duty of working full-time and squeezing in a part-time job while attending night school three times a week, so I could complete my degree. By knowing that failure was not an option because my son's life depended on me – I uncovered an untapped reservoir of determination and resilience.

Between the coffee refills and tired yawns of late night studying, moments of illumination started emerging from the hectic rhythm of my life. I was discovering the power of my own potential. *The pursuit of knowledge and personal growth was opening doors to a world of possibilities. A fire was awakening within me defying all expectations. I was beginning to carve my very own path.

Navigating a Changing Landscape

Amidst my personal journey, the external landscape of society was undergoing profound transformation. It was the mid-1980s and a significant social shift was beginning. Women were "reclaiming" their power and challenging the traditional norms. As a single mother trying to create a better life for my son, I found myself navigating these *external* changes at the same time I was confronting my own *internal* struggles.

During this era, women were breaking free from the chains of inequality. Legal advancements granted women rights that we take for granted today. Women were now allowed to open their own banking accounts and apply for mortgages without a male co-signer. Women were increasingly entering the workforce and defying many other societal expectations. They were asserting their skills and talents in a male-dominated world. However, all this newfound empowerment came so quickly no one had the tools or wisdom of how to deal with it, so it actually created its own set of challenges and internal conflicts for both men and women alike.

The changing expectations and roles in society gave many men an identity crisis. Since the beginning of time it seemed civilization put emphasis and worth on a man's ability to provide for his family. His masculinity was tied with being the breadwinner. When women started entering a male-dominated workforce and becoming breadwinners themselves, many men struggled to keep up with the changing dynamics. Some men felt their very character and purpose were being threatened, and an uncertain era began.

There were many more implications for both men and women than just in the workforce. Some men felt a sense of emasculation and inadequacy, and were forced to re-evaluate deep personal values and beliefs when it came to the changing gender roles at home. It was extremely hard for many to take on what was once considered the feminine role of childcare and household chores and let go of traditional ways that were now being called "old-fashioned." There was also a shift for men when it came to their emotions. Before this time men were discouraged to show too much emotional expression and vulnerability. Many times they forced and trained themselves to hold back their feelings. Now they were being encouraged to open up and share their emotions. It wasn't an easy switch and still to this day it is not accepted by a large portion of men.

Author's note: The feminine role for men has come so far. Recently my son was taking his son to swimming lessons. I went and watched. I was truly astonished at the family changing room, and how involved the fathers were, but also that it was almost all men in the pool. That was unheard of when I raised my son, and it felt good to see men embracing the important role of fatherhood. My generation had so many men walk away and leave women to raise kids on their own.

For many women, all of these changes came with a high price. At this time, not only were a vast majority of them still the one and only in their married partnership that did all of the cooking, cleaning, sewing, and so on . . . now in this new and shifting culture they were also expected to share the responsibility of earning an income. Once they were hired into this male dominated workforce, the troubles were just beginning.

They faced gender discrimination; after all, it was thought that a woman's income was just supporting her husband's so there was no need for women to get paid the same as a man. There were very limited opportunities for advancement, and many barriers, biases, and blocks that made their professional journeys more difficult than those of their male counterparts.

Another huge problem for women in the workplace during this era was unwanted sexual advances and harassment. Unwelcomed, demeaning comments and discriminatory treatment were unfortunately very common. Women who experienced this harassment really had limited avenues for support or legal protection at that time. There was really no one to whom they could go for advice concerning the countless problems they faced because of the rarity of women in the workforce and leadership positions.

I was a young woman and a brand new mom during this time. For me the internal struggles of integrating society's expectations with my own personal identity added an extra layer of complexity to my journey. As women stepped into the professional sphere, I felt a pressure to cast off traditional feminine attributes and embrace more masculine traits in order to succeed. This was a complex balancing act, attempting to find a perfect sweet-spot where femininity and cold hard strength could co-exist harmoniously.

As if life couldn't get any more confusing and difficult, enter the emergence of new technological advancements. Another more high-tech transformation was beginning to take hold at this time as well. Debit cards, credit cards and consumerism began permeating our culture and transforming our relationship with money and material possessions to a disproportionate level, something that had never before been experienced.

The personal computer was also emerging at this same time, changing the way people navigated the vast realm of information and paving a new way people would connect to one another. The internet was developing, and beginning to reshape our entire world. The way we interacted with one another, and ultimately how we maneuvered the world, was forever changed.

During this era of rampant transitions and contradictions I encountered many internal conflicts that tested the very core of my being, forcing me to question and redefine my own true beliefs. Old structures held strong and tight while new possibilities beckoned me onward. As I continued to pursue my personal growth it became increasingly challenging to muddle through all of my conflicting beliefs, as well as society's shifting tides of new expectations.

I quickly realized that the knowledge I was acquiring through the traditional education system had a short shelf life. The rapid pace of change rendered much of what I learned obsolete and irrelevant before I was even able to put it into practice. It became evident to me that if I wanted to not only survive – but really thrive – in this ever-evolving world, I needed to take control of my own education and embark on a journey of personal growth. It was past time for me to begin actively seeking sources for personal transformation and self- awareness.

Because of my fierce determination to provide a brighter future for my son, I refused to succumb to the limitations of traditional learning. I made an unbendable decision to become captain of my own education ship. I clearly knew that I had to break free from the confines of the classroom and embrace alternative avenues that would empower me with relevant and practical knowledge.

In Eastern philosophy there is an old expression that states, "When the student is ready, the master will appear." I was ready to receive wisdom and guidance, and the appropriate teacher appeared miraculously one Saturday night on an infomercial. Tony Robbins.

His charisma immediately ignited a spark within me. Offering me a different mindset than I had heard before, he gave me hope for limitless possibilities and personal transformation. I was completely intrigued. I absorbed as much as I could from his free teachings on TV, and eagerly invested in his courses. This was my first step into the world of alternative education and self- improvement.

Author's note: This moment for me can serve as a reminder and guide for you. The importance of being open and receptive for learning and growth is the way to acquire the knowledge you yearn for. It will help you develop the qualities in yourself you desire, and the right opportunities and mentors will present themselves to you. You don't have to work at finding them. And some unsolicited advice for any new mothers reading this - trust your instincts and your heart. You were designed to raise this child. You don't have to follow the rules, books, or opinions of others unless they resonate with you.

One of my favorite things that I learned from Tony Robbins was when he would walk for miles, the whole time repeating over and over, "Every day in every way – I'm getting better and better." This was my first clue that I had power over my life. I was coming to realize that I was the one in charge of my life. I had the power deep inside me to change my beliefs and my brain. But what was it that I truly believed? Did family really come first? What role did a good woman play in order to keep peace?

On the weekends my searching led me to what is now called "binge watching" public television programs on topics such as social conditioning, human behavior, and the incredible potential we all possess. These weekend deep dives with world renowned teachers such as Dr. Wayne Dyer and Dr. Daniel Amen expanded my understanding of the power of the mind, and its endless capacity for personal growth. Through these televised encounters I began grasping the concept of becoming the best version of myself. Wayne and Daniel were empowering me with a notion that resonated deeply within my soul. I started recognizing the immense potential within us all. As I absorbed these transformative teachings, it became clear and evident that the key to unlocking my true potential lay in embracing self-development and cultivating a growth mindset.

T. Harv Eker taught me the importance of developing a "wealthy mindset" to achieve financial success. Through his teachings I was beginning to grasp the idea of how much our thoughts and beliefs around money greatly impact our ability to create wealth. I knew I needed to overcome some limiting beliefs regarding money, in order to attract it to me.

I actually started hiding money from myself in an effort to take control of it. My outside surroundings weren't agreeing with all of the internal changes I was making. It was like trying to run in quicksand. I kept getting sucked back into my old beliefs and habit patterns.

Interestingly I had an "aha" moment one day. For most of millennia people didn't really know that they were surrendering or possibly out of alignment to what they truly wanted in life. As long as all of their needs were being met, they were in a good place. It was quite a job a thousand years ago just taking care of the basics like food, shelter, and clothing. They literally had to have a hand in everything that was needed to survive. Today, we can just go to a store and buy our food and clothing. We shop around and purchase the house or rent an apartment. There are no animals to kill or trees to fell. It's all right there, so we have more time to think about what it is we really want and truly desire. When we look around and realize that life isn't as amazing as it could be, we get depressed or annoyed – maybe even a bit angry. We try using our willpower and strength like they did hundreds of years ago to get what we want. But we just go in circles, pushing our way through. We've been programmed to believe that is the way to success, but it actually keeps us in our current situation.

After completing Tony Robbins' course I met my first mentor, T. Harv Eker. His groundbreaking program called the Millionaire Mind was a game changer for me. It was even free, except for the small investment of meals and accommodations. For anyone wishing to uncover their true relationship to money I wholeheartedly recommend attending this workshop. It was there that I learned that the biggest obstacle to wealth is fear. People are afraid of thinking big. The only problem is that if you think small you'll only achieve small things. Money is not the real goal. The real goal is freedom. Money is just a tool to help you live your life the way you truly desire.

During this Millionaire Mind weekend we were provided with a profound mirror, allowing us to explore the deep-seated beliefs and conditioning we were holding around wealth and abundance. It served as a powerful tool for self-reflection, revealing the subconscious programming that influenced our thoughts, emotions, and actions regarding money; he called this our "money blueprint." Through this experience I gained invaluable insights into my own money mindset, and then I began the transformative process of rewiring my brain for financial success.

Now I was on my way to effectively managing money. I learned how to trade in the stock market, and I was good at it. Looking back it seems to me that whether you're designing a trading plan, designing a home or designing a life, they all work the same way with personal knowledge of the self.

As I delved deeper into the workings of the human mind I started seeking answers to profound questions that stirred within me. The teachings of esteemed experts like Dr. Bruce Lipton and Dr. Daniel Amen shed light on the incredible power of my subconscious mind. I began uncovering the facts about subconscious programming, and how it is intricately linked to the interpretations of our experiences. I learned that we actually form beliefs based on our interpretations of every event that happens in our lives. This creates a roadmap for our future, influencing all of our thoughts, feelings and actions – and ultimately every result or experience.

The conscious mind, which operates at the forefront of our awareness, accounts for a mere five percent of our mental activity. In contrast, the subconscious mind tirelessly orchestrates the remaining ninety-five percent – working tirelessly around the clock and in the background on autopilot. Think about this for a moment. Isn't it incredible that you never have to tell your lungs to breathe? Or your heart to beat. If you play the piano or pitch for a baseball team you most likely do best when you are on autopilot and allow your subconscious mind to take control.

This is an essential aspect of understanding the power of the subconscious mind and recognizing the intricate connection between our minds and bodies. Our bodies function as remarkable biomechanical beings designed for optimal efficiency. This division of labor allows our conscious mind to focus on intellectual growth and expansion.

Did you know that within the vast domain of the subconscious, our brains actually create and utilize efficiency recipes? These so-called recipes are pre- programmed responses that dictate our every action. When specific triggers occur, it's a result of a past experience and the interpretations we assigned to it. Understanding these efficiency recipes that usually operate outside of our conscious awareness, and being aware of how those deep-rooted patterns shape our behavior, grants us the power to re-evaluate and modify our subconscious programming. This enables us to align our actions with our desired outcomes. Think of this for a moment: ninety-five percent of our brain is processed by the unconscious mind. This division of labor allows our conscious minds to focus on intellectual growth and expansion.

So where did all of this subconscious programming and these brain recipes come from? How did all of this disempowering information get stuck inside the brains of almost everyone around the world? In order to gain this understanding we have to go way back in history – back to the time when the Roman Empire was crumbling.

This point in history is often called the "Dark Ages" or "Medieval Ages." The term "Dark Ages" doesn't refer to lack of cultural or intellectual progress, but refers to the decline of a centralized governance and economic stability. Also, little is known of this time because of the lack of historical documentation compared to when the Romans ruled.

During this era, Europe was experiencing significant political, social and economic changes. Feudalism and feudal kingdoms, the rise of Christianity and the spread of Islam played important roles. At the same time various developments in areas such as art, architecture, literature, and intellectual pursuits were sought. The groundwork for the Renaissance period was being laid.

The loss of authority from the centralized Roman government and infrastructure left a complete and total power vacuum. Barbarian kingdoms of Germanic tribes, once part of the Roman Empire, took advantage of the absence of authority and carved out their own realms. The Byzantine Empire continued to exist and kept much of the Roman culture, but with the rise of Islam vast territories of the Byzantines were conquered. The hierarchical system of Feudalism was not pleasant for the ones deemed as peasants, but provided the framework for governance and social order during this time of chaos.

The Catholic Church played a vital role in preserving the culture and knowledge of that time. They developed monasteries and scriptoria (writing rooms) within the church and were responsible for copying and preserving ancient texts, including works of literature, philosophy, and religious writings. It was the most dominant religious institution in Europe offering hope and salvation in an uncertain world. Many of the Catholic communities of this time were involved in charitable affairs providing relief to the poor, establishing hospitals, and building schools. The church was so powerful at this period they influenced and governed even over secular rulers − not to mention the many monarchies that bowed down to the Catholic Church, recognizing its moral authority and thus submitting to its rule. Even though the church's actions and rulings in many cases followed the rules of kindness and love that they preached, many other times these rulings could be corrupt and immoral.

This convergence of spiritual and political power fit perfectly into the feudal system and hierarchical control. Limiting opportunities and disempowering the masses. With the church assuming the role of both ruler and spiritual guide it could wield total control over the lives of almost everyone. While the church dictated the moral codes, laws and social behaviors, it was accruing massive wealth through various means. Some of these ways were perfectly moral and some on the sinful side from the church's very own standards. With the accumulation of wealth, the church's position of influence and power was a dominant force throughout most of the world.

Monarchies maintained their grip on political power and imposed burdensome taxation over their poverty-stricken peasants to ensure their reign of power would last for generations. This socioeconomic structure perpetuated a cycle of total disempowerment for the masses, and forced them to become dependent upon all those who were in positions of authority. This oppressive grip of the ruling class be it the monarchies or the church stifled individual independence and hindered communal development.

It is said that within every problem and challenge the seeds of solutions are sown. The average person might have been held down by those in authority, but this discontent ignited a yearning for freedom and individuality, and the opportunity to shape one's own destiny. Thousands of years later the remnants of the social structure established after the fall of the Roman Empire continue to influence our lives and shape our perceptions today.

Another very significant thing that happened during this time was in the field of medicine. Medical science was advancing faster than many people could keep up with – especially those in the church. The church believed in the sanctity of the human body; this belief was hindering the progress and understanding of human anatomy and physiology. After persistent efforts by doctors and medical practitioners the church reluctantly started allowing autopsies to provide insights to how the human body actually worked. But this came with a stipulation – science controlled the body, and the church controlled the spirit and mind. This separation of body/mind/spirit is one of the reasons we have a fragmentation of human existence. It reinforced the notion that the body, mind, and spirit are distinct entities that should be treated separately.

As if this wasn't enough, throw Sir Isaac Newton into the mix. His revolutionary discoveries of the laws of motion and universal gravitation had a profound impact on the way we perceive the physical world. Next came the belief that everything could be broken down into its smallest physical components and explained and clarified. This led to a paradigm shift that only the tangible, measurable, and physical aspects of reality had significance; while intangible qualities such as imagination, intuition, and creativity were considered irrelevant.

As a consequence, the interconnectedness of various aspects of life was overlooked. Leading to a disconnection between different domains of knowledge. (You stay in your field – I'll stay in mine and we don't share knowledge.) The immeasurable and profound significance of intuition, imagination, and creativity was passed over in favor of the purely tangible attributes.

This separation between body, mind, and spirit has influenced our perception of how we treat our bodies today. The "holistic approach" is considered "non- traditional" and a little on the fringe in today's society, but by acknowledging this historical context we can begin embracing a more well-rounded and integrated, holistic approach to our personal health and personal mindset.

The groundwork of history is laid. Now, fast forward a few hundred years to the beginning of the twentieth century. The start of the 1900's marked the introduction of the Industrial Revolution, changing the way we lived, worked, and related to one another. Manual labor and craftsmanship went to being mechanized, mass manufacturing. Items that were handmade with skill and craftsmanship were now completely devalued. It was all about speed, efficiency and mass production. Because of this a massive workforce was needed to operate the machinery and new industries. Individuals were enticed to leave their families and neighbors with a promise of a secure and steady income. People migrated in droves to towns and big cities to have this promise of riches fulfilled.

Now the communal ties were broken. No longer did people know and love their neighbors. Families were separated from each other, and the emergence of isolation and self-centered societies was born. The focus was now more about material wealth than a loved one. Within the industrial workplaces themselves, jobs became increasingly specialized and divided. The pursuit of efficiency and productivity led to the compartmentalization of tasks, with workers assigned narrow roles that required repetitive and monotonous actions. This specialization further fragmented the workforce and limited individuals' opportunities for personal growth and development beyond their assigned roles.

The industrial revolution revealed a need for a different method of educating children. Farmers and craftsmen didn't make good factory workers. To fulfill this need the government established public schools. This way the emerging workforce could be educated the way they needed to be. The educational system that emerged during this period was largely influenced by the interests of big business owners and the government, aiming to produce compliant and conforming individuals rather than nurturing personal empowerment, creativity, and critical thinking.

Conformity, uniformity, and the judgment of subjective grading systems became prevalent within the education system. Nonconformity and alternative perspectives were often condemned, leading to the perception that those who did not fit the mold were deemed unwell or in need of modification so as to conform to societal norms. Crucial aspects of personal development, such as financial literacy, personal empowerment, creative expression, and critical thinking, were often overlooked or excluded from the curriculum, as they did not align with the workforce needs defined by the business owners and government.

Now that you know why your subconscious comes up with the brain recipes that it does – it's time that you start reclaiming your individuality and fostering your creativity. Embracing alternative perspectives and nurturing critical thinking. Let's start transcending the limitations imposed upon us for millennia and forge a path towards fulfillment, empowerment, and holistic understanding of ourselves and the world around us. Let's bridge the gap between the physical and non-physical aspects of our existence, explore the interconnectedness of knowledge, and embrace a more profound and meaningful understanding of ourselves and the world around us.

This takes us to the 1920's on the timeline of life, when a remarkable scientific breakthrough occurred with the emergence of quantum physics. This field of study is revolutionary to our understanding of the ultimate nature of reality. It challenges the conventional Newtonian physics and opens up a new realm of possibilities.

It seems that since time began, advancements in science and technology were primarily driven by business interests and the pursuit of profitability. Cell phones, computers, MRI machines, and satellites, just to name a few, have reshaped our lives dramatically. They have literally transformed our society. But there was a piece of the puzzle missing that most didn't even know wasn't there. It was the profound effect of quantum physics on everything and everyone.

Quantum physics reveals a fascinating truth: what was once thought as empty space or nothingness is actually pure energy. Energy, as revealed by quantum physics, cannot be created or destroyed; it can only change form. This understanding revolutionizes how we see the world and ourselves.

If we are to think deeply, we understand that there is much more to us than what we can see on the outside. When we dive deeply into the depth of our beings, we discover that we are pure energy. We are literally energy beings. This is what makes us intricately interconnected with the entire universe, because the driving force of the physical world is actually energy. The boundaries we notice are really just illusions. Energy knows no separation. To be sure, there are different vibrations and frequencies that give our world diversity – but truly everything and everyone is connected through energy.

You must admit that there are many stories that you have heard that cannot be explained by the old Newtonian physics. For example, you can be in a room with a couple of people enjoying each other's company and all of a sudden someone enters the same room in a bad mood. Even if they don't say or do anything, you can feel the change in energy.

Recognizing the far-reaching and unifying consequences of energy over your life will give an incentive to embrace a more holistic perspective. We are not separate from our environment, nor are we separate from one another. The interchange of energy creates a tapestry of relationships among all people, places and things. Our thoughts, emotions and actions echo through the energetic network that permeates our existence.

By aligning ourselves with the principles of quantum physics, we can tap into the inherent power of energy. We can consciously shape our reality, recognizing that our intentions and vibrations have the potential to influence our outcomes and experiences. Are you ready to be empowered and transcend limitations? Are you ready to embark on an incredible and transformative journey? Keep reading to find the answers to these questions and embark on a transformative spiritual journey of self-discovery and growth.

Did you know that you are made of the same cosmic material as your Creator? You are not separate from the universe − you are instead an integral part of it. Your body, mind and spirit are intertwined with eight billion others. You are constantly in a delicate dance of interconnectedness.

There is great power that resides within you. As you read these words you are pulsating with the force of life. You literally have infinite potential. Take the time now to start unraveling and unlearning those outdated beliefs that no longer serve you. The ones that have limited your power by telling you that you were small and insignificant.

Begin this moment to step into your natural and internal power. Shake off and shed the shackles of societal conditioning. Unlock the dormant potential residing within. Reclaim your sovereignty. Embrace the fullness of you.

Connecting to the Divine Self is not always an easy journey. Those deeply ingrained beliefs and societal norms are strong. But embarking on the path of personal transformation has immense rewards. Shedding layers of illusions helps us remember our inborn and natural connection to the Divine Intelligence that permeates and penetrates all of creation.

Aligning our thoughts, emotions, and actions with our highest truth is the first step to becoming co-creators of our reality. This gives us the leadership role of actively participating in the unfolding of our lives and that of the collective consciousness. Through this self-awareness of intention and conscious choice we shape our own destiny by sewing the threads of our own choice to the great tapestry of life.

Embrace your wholeness. Recognize that you are not a small fragmented part of this earth, but instead are an integral interconnected expression of the Divine. Choose to make a contribution to the transformation of our world by infusing it with love, compassion and conscious evolution.

What will your contribution be?

"Where globalization means, as it so often does, that the rich and powerful now have new means to further enrich and empower themselves at the cost of the poorer and weaker, we have a responsibility to protest in the name of universal freedom."
—Nelson Mandela

Lawyer, politician, and activist in South Africa, who was imprisoned for 27 years. Upon his release he became the first Black President.

CHAPTER 2

The Truth About the Personal Power
You Have Always Had

Your body is always speaking to you, but you really have no idea of what it's saying. Don't you think it's time to Learn the Language?

Exciting new discoveries in science reveal that our bodies are *always* communicating with us, using a distinctive language that doesn't involve any words. Can you imagine having a two-way conversation with your own body? Our bodies combine electromagnetic, biochemical, and mechanical elements – just like the world we live in. Understanding this opens up amazing possibilities. These things were not taught to us in school, at home, or even in church. These places taught us how to fit into the social structure, but many times left out a more important aspect of living in alignment – and that is self- empowerment. Knowing how to trust ourselves. The saying trust your heart has been around forever. It mainly just supplies lip-service to the truth. I will show you how to put those words to the test and really teach you how to "trust your heart."

The old ways of living that didn't serve us as individuals or as a society are no longer sustainable. We are witnessing the crumbling of old systems all around us. But don't worry, there's hope! My mission is to share this knowledge and help as many people as possible embrace their greatness. How? By teaching you the language of your body, showing you how to Unlearn the Crap, and reprogram your mind.

Your dreams and desires are not mere fantasies; they are powerful guides, leading you in the right direction. Trusting them is not selfish – it's the key to discovering your true path and purpose in life. So, let's get together and follow those dreams, listen to your body and create a better, more fulfilling future for yourself and others. Together, we will embark on an incredible journey of growth and transformation.

So what exactly is this special language that our bodies speak? You might think It's some kind of secret code, but really it's a mixture of sensations, emotions and gut feelings that guide us through life's adventures. Our bodies are like a superhero sidekick, constantly telling us about the environment we're in and giving us tips on how to be our best selves. We are biomechanical, electro- magnetic, energetic beings. This is not woowoo – it is science and physics.

North American Indians were taught this deep connection that we have to nature, and the holistic understanding of health and well-being. They put an emphasis on listening to their body and paying attention to physical, emotional, and spiritual cues to understand what might be ailing them. Their traditional practices often involve a blending of physical remedies, herbal medicine, spiritual rituals, and a close relationship with the natural world. For example, Native American healing practices frequently incorporate the concept of balance and harmony between the individual, the community, and the environment. Illness is seen as a result of imbalance in these three aspects of life. For many indigenous cultures a more holistic approach is used. Physical symptoms are not the only ones addressed, but also emotional and spiritual, for the complete well-being of the individual.

To understand this language all you have to do is tune in and listen. When you do this your senses become body whisperers telling you everything you need to know. Your body is a messenger, relaying insights, warnings, and guidance. It possesses an innate wisdom that goes beyond your intellectual understanding. You can pick up on all of those subtle signals, vibes, and little hints that only your body can feel, by using your intuition.

Our bodies are very chatty, but they are also very wise. They have a library of wisdom that goes well beyond textbooks and facts. Our bodies know how to tap into the grand database of life because they are interconnected and in constant communication with our environment. They are constantly responding to stimuli and sending us messages that guide us towards optimal well-being and alignment.

Cracking this code that the body speaks unlocks a treasure trove of insight and growth, leading to an epic journey of self-discovery. By speaking the language of your body you create an unbreakable bond between your thoughts, your physical being, and your soul. It's a magical connection that nourishes your whole being.

Are you ready to start honoring your body? Listen closely. What is it trying to tell you at this moment? Are you hungry, tired, excited? Let your inner wisdom be the guide. Turn up the volume and listen closely to that internal conversation that you have been ignoring up until now.

It's time to unleash your greatness. Begin by paying very close attention to your dreams. These are not just wild fantasies – your soul is actually talking to you. Your dreams are like a compass guiding you to your true purpose. It's very important not to just brush them off. They play a significant role in unlocking your full potential.

Just knowing this can be a complete game-changer. Let the old rules that once held you back fall apart at the seams. Let go of what doesn't serve you by listening to your body and how it feels when you think about certain things, and embrace those things that make you feel happy and uplift your spirit.

Shedding the old conditioning helps rewrite the script in your mind, and then you become the author of your destiny. Create a life for yourself that dances with and is in sync with your inner essence.

To really understand the code that your body is using you need to be aware of a fact that most people have never heard of. Brace yourself . . . you actually have THREE brains! Yes, it's true; and I will repeat it so it starts to sink in . . . you actually have THREE brains!

Unlike conventional thinking we do not have one central intelligence system in our body. We are actually a tri-brained superpower. Each of our brains uses different intelligence to process different information and send the messages back and forth between the other two brains.

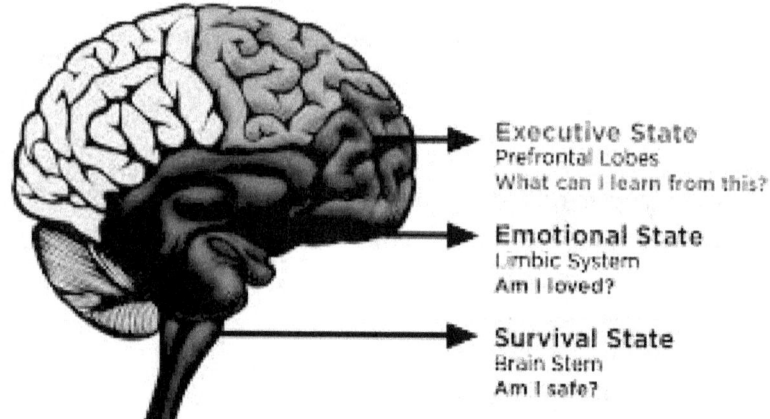

https://steemit.com/life/@joehedz/triune-brain-sin-and-the-behaviour-of-human

Brain #1 — The Brain in Our Head, and Its Three Process Systems

This is the brain we all think is our only brain. The one in our head. It has **three distinct processes and functions** that have evolved with our environment. All information and stimulus must follow the flow sequence for information to be processed.

The first process resides in the primal brain – which can be found at the base of our neck and central nervous system. This is the ancient brain, inherited from our prehistoric ancestors.

Its mission is asking, "Am I safe?"

It scans billions of data bytes, looking out for danger. If it spots trouble, it sounds the alarm, and our central nervous system takes charge. If there is no danger then the information gets passed to the next part of our brain – the emotional part.

The second process is that of the emotional brain, which covers the primal brain. This is the brain's programming center because emotions are the keys to our programs.

Its mission is asking, "Am I loved?

This part of the brain records all of our experiences, which creates a treasure trove of emotions. Every situation gets a special emotional response that becomes our triggers. It's like our body's autopilot. This is why sometimes we react without even knowing why. We don't realize it because everything is already in motion and it has not yet moved into the intellectual part of our brain.

The third process is that of the intellectual brain – which covers both other brains and expands into our forehead area. This was the last part of our brain to evolve and only once survival systems were in place.

Its mission is asking, "Am I important, and do I matter?"

This is the mastermind behind all the amazing, creative, inventive and troubleshooting ideas to make life meaningful. The intellectual brain serves as a powerhouse of cognitive capabilities, expanding our capacity to analyze, synthesize, and derive insights from the world around us. It is here that we engage in critical thinking, utilizing logic, and employ our creative faculties to envision new possibilities, develop innovative solutions, and explore the depths of our human potential.

We innately seek to understand our place in the world. We really want to make a difference, and to contribute to something greater than ourselves. It is through this pursuit of personal importance that we uncover our unique gifts, talents, and passions, allowing us to make meaningful contributions to the tapestry of existence.

The intellectual brain is not limited to the realm of intellect alone; it is intimately connected to our emotional landscape. It is through the integration of our thoughts and emotions that we gain a deeper understanding of our true desires and aspirations. This integration guides us in aligning our intellectual pursuits with our authentic values, creating a sense of purpose and fulfillment in our lives.

By nurturing the intellectual brain, we embark on a journey of self-discovery, self-expression and personal growth. We realize that our thoughts have the power to shape our reality and impact our world. It is here that we tap into our innate potential and unravel the mysteries of the universe.

By recognizing and understanding the roles of these three brain process systems, we gain insights into the intricate workings of our mind-body system. We comprehend how our primal brain assesses threats and safeguards our survival, how our emotional brain stores and triggers programmed responses, and how our intelligence brain allows us to think, reason, and make conscious choices.

But there is more to the brain that we all know and love than these three functions – there is also a conscious and a subconscious mind. The unconscious mind is behind the scenes doing all the things we need to survive but don't even remember we're doing them. It actually handles ninety-five percent of our lives. It's like our brain's own personal assistant. It automates everything, from our bodily functions to our thoughts and actions. It stores all of our beliefs – even if they're not always in our best interest, because its only focus is to be right. If the programming in the subconscious mind were to be wrong it could prove to be catastrophic. That's why changing our beliefs can be really tough.

The thought of going on a diet and getting healthy is processed by both the conscious and unconscious mind. They do not communicate well. Remember the subconscious only wants to be right – *I believe the subconscious mind is our ego.* In fact, the subconscious mind is only designed to be right. It's not designed to be happy, wealthy, healthy, or successful – only right. So, the only way to successfully change our lives is by changing the subconscious beliefs and programming.

The good news is that science has now proven within the study of neuroplasticity, NLP (neuro-linguistic programming), and many other healing modalities, that we do indeed have the power to change our beliefs. Neuroplasticity helps forge new pathways, while NLP lets us reframe experiences. And it can be done in an instant. If you think it takes time and progress, then you haven't arrived at a true place of decision. Decision is the way you change your beliefs, your thoughts and your life, but you must be firm and resolute. It's all about rewiring your brain.

This is how we transform. First we need to tap into the subconscious mind and open the hidden treasure chest filled with all of the beliefs that have shaped our thoughts, emotions, and actions. These beliefs are not fixed but malleable. Conscious awareness is the key that opens the subconscious mind. Mindfulness and self-reflection will help. Ask yourself questions like, "Do these old ideas still serve?" By doing this you can disrupt those old patterns and make a change.

With dedication and proven methods, you can reprogram your unconscious mind and align with your beliefs and wildest dreams. The power is truly within you. Embrace the realm of decision to align with your highest vision.

Author's note: I have studied and conquered these methods, and I would love to help you understand how to do this. If you would like more information on neuroplasticity or NLP, please see reference at the end of this book on my Rise Up Coaching Program. www.RiseUpCoaching.io

Neuroplasticity, through the rewiring of neural connections, allows us to forge new pathways and patterns of thought. NLP techniques provide us with practical tools to reframe our experiences, communicate effectively, and harness the power of language to shape our reality. These modalities, among others, enable us to access our inner potential and create transformative shifts with remarkable speed and efficacy. In the journey of transforming our beliefs, decision emerges as the driving force that propels us towards our desired outcomes.

Brain #2 — Our Heart

This brain is what we call our heart. It's much more than a mechanical pump. It has an intelligence system all its own. The Heartmath Institute has been studying the heart for decades and they've found some mind-blowing insights. Your heart actually sends and receives signals and information from the outside world even before the other brains are aware of anything. It takes in information and sends it to the other brains very quickly – even *before* the event has come to your attention.

Our heart sends and receives signals and information to and from the brain and other parts of our bodies to set in motion their part of the program that needs to be activated by the emotional brain. It does this with an electrical current, which can actually be measured on an electrocardiogram machine (ECG). This current not only travels through our bodies but can be measured more than three feet beyond our bodies. That is how our heart gains the information before our intellectual or emotional brains. Our heart is connecting with all of the energy around us before we even get there. It's like a cosmic Wi-Fi hotspot.

Besides being able to process and send information and instruction to our other brains, the heart has an incredible memory. Heart transplant recipients have shared memories and traits from their donors. Like knowing places they have never been or languages they have never heard. Even tastes for things they have never had. Did you know that once a murderer was caught only because of the memory of the heart of the victim? A girl was murdered. Her heart was given to another child. This child was able to share enough information about the murder that the authorities were able to convict the killer. The information given was only available to the victim.

This extraordinary account illuminates the intricate web of connections and intelligence within our being. The heart serves as a repository of experiences, wisdom, and energetic imprints, defying traditional notions of localized memory storage. It invites us to explore the vast depths of our inter- connectedness, and the boundless possibilities that lie within.

Recognizing and honoring the heart's intelligence allows us to forge a deeper connection with ourselves and the world around us. By cultivating practices such as heart coherence, compassion, and gratitude, we can tap into the heart's inherent wisdom and expand our capacity for empathy, love, and connection. Through the integration of the heart's wisdom we embark on a path of wholeness and authenticity.

Brain #3 — Our Gut

This brain is our most primal brain and located in the gut. Our digestive system may seem simple, but it's really not simple at all. Yes, it takes in, processes, and eliminates food for survival, but as the brains of the mind and heart evolved so did the gut.

There are millions of tiny, little, powerful microbiomes inside your gut making sure you stay healthy and happy. These microbiomes can even control your cravings and influence your behavior. They are like little gut detectives. But if there is a parasite in your gut it can actually send signals to the brain that will make you do things that are only in the best interest of the parasite. It is even strong enough to take control for its own survival even if it means making you sacrifice your own best interest.

There are specific microbiomes that are associated with weight control. We used to say it was our genes or DNA that made us overweight and we had no control over the situation. In some ways there is a bit of truth to that, but scientists have discovered that overweight people are lacking some of the microbiomes that thin people have.

The gut is often one of the first places we feel things. The saying "My gut hurts," or "I feel like I got punched in the gut" can literally be how we feel when we are upset over something.

Our gut is a complex ecosystem of microbiomes. We have more microbiomes in our gut than we have in our DNA strands, and it's way more complex than our DNA structure. It's like a command center for our health and survival. Scientists are finding connections between gut health and diseases like Parkinson's and Alzheimer's; these diseases could actually be caused by digestive issues. It has been discovered that the gut is actually the first place where disease is created. It is from the direct results of stress and inflammation that most diseases have their origin, and this starts in the gut.

By recognizing the power and complexity of our gut, we can embark on a journey of holistic well-being. Nurturing the microbiomes within our gut through a balanced, nutritious diet, stress management, and mindful practices fosters a harmonious relationship between our gut, brain, and heart. This interconnectedness contributes to optimal health, vitality, and the prevention of diseases that may originate within the gut.

The Central Nervous System

All of the sharing of information between the brains would be impossible without the central nervous system. Our central nervous system can be thought of as a switching station. The **on switch is called the sympathetic nervous system** and the **off switch is called the parasympathetic nervous system**. It takes its orders mainly from the primal brain to turn on. Once the primal brain rings the bell of danger, then the central nervous system turns on the switch. A whole series of actions are done internally through our electric nerve system, our hormonal biochemical system and our mechanical systems. Anything that is needed to get us out of danger is heightened and anything that is not necessary for immediate survival is almost shut down. Let me explain. When the danger bell rings, our stress hormones are released into our system which then sets off a whole series of events. Our breathing gets fast and shallow, our heart begins to race, our body is alive with energy, and there are hormones sent to our muscles so we can physically handle the danger. On the other hand, we do not need to think or be logical, so our intellectual mind is reduced, we do not need to process food immediately so our digestion is stopped. Only that which will get us to safety has priority in resources.

Once we are out of danger and the all clear signal is released, then our parasympathetic system kicks in and returns us to homeostasis (technical word for balance). We are supposed to be in this state the majority of our time, only turning on the danger switch if there is a threat to our survival. Unfortunately our central nervous system doesn't know the difference between a tiger or a bad driver that cuts us off. It doesn't know if we are being threatened with bodily harm or if we thought someone offended us.

It is literally either ON or OFF.

But this orchestrated response shows the incredible adaptability and efficiency of our body's survival mechanisms. It demonstrates how our innate intelligence prioritizes resources, ensuring the distribution of energy to essential survival functions.

Even though these processes happen automatically, it doesn't mean we're powerless. In fact, we have the incredible ability to influence and even flip the switch intentionally. By tapping into our subconscious mind and practicing with dedication and repetition, we gain control over these processes. It's like mastering a skill that empowers us to shape our own experiences and responses. The power is in our hands.

Understanding the interplay between the sympathetic and parasympathetic nervous systems allows us to direct our body's response to stress and create conditions for optimal well-being. By activating the off switch—the parasympathetic nervous system—we can restore a state of calm and equilibrium, allowing our body to heal, repair, and engage in essential functions such as digestion, rest, and rejuvenation.

When we practice self-care and self-regulation by harmonizing the sympathetic and parasympathetic responses, we unlock the potential for greater resilience, vitality, and a profound connection with the innate intelligence that resides within us. Practicing flipping the switch consciously gives us greater control over our stress responses, promoting well-being, resilience, and emotional balance.

Through practices such as deep breathing, mindfulness, meditation, and stress-reducing techniques, we actively take part in our body's switching station, supporting balance and developing a sense of inner harmony. By consciously improving a parasympathetic response, we empower ourselves to counteract the harmful effects of chronic stress, creating an environment conducive to overall well-being.

When we purposefully engage with our subconscious mind, we initiate a profound dance between conscious intent and the innate intelligence residing within us. By reprogramming our automatic responses, we can cultivate a heightened sense of self-awareness, influencing our body's physiological and emotional states.

Thirty-three Senses

Our senses are the way we bring information into ourselves. They process the outside stimuli and inform our brains on what is happening. We have been brought up to believe that we have only five senses: hearing, sight, taste, touch, and smell. These are only our basic senses. Some researchers and scholars propose we have as many as thirty-three different senses. The concept of senses can vary depending on how they are defined. Some are more physiological and others are more cognitive.

Here are a few examples:

1. **Proprioception**: This is the sense of the relative position and movement of body parts. It allows you to know where your body is in space without having to look at it.

2. **Equilibrioception**: Also known as the sense of balance, this helps you maintain your body's balance and orientation.

3. **Nociception**: This is the ability to perceive pain. It alerts you to potential damage or injury to your body.

4. **Thermoception**: This is the sense of temperature. It allows you to perceive hot and cold sensations.

5. **Chronoception**: The sense of time passing. It helps you perceive the passage of time and intervals between events.

6. **Interoception**: The ability to sense the internal state of your body, including sensations related to hunger, thirst, heartbeat, and more.

7. **Magnetoception**: Some animals are believed to possess the ability to sense the earth's magnetic field, helping them navigate over long distances.

8. **Stretch Receptors**: These receptors in your muscles and joints allow you to sense the degree of stretch in your body, contributing to your body's spatial awareness.

Flavor is an example of sensory interaction: what we call the "taste" of food mainly comes from smell rather than taste buds. A loss of smell will greatly affect one's eating experience. Try holding your nose while you eat an onion. If you were truly able to do this you would have a hard time distinguishing it from an apple. Flavor experiences are also affected by color, three-dimensional arrangements and even sounds. These examples demonstrate that multi- sensory interactions are the rule rather than the exception.

These additional senses encompass a wide range of abilities, providing us with unique avenues to interact with and understand the world around us. These expanded senses offer us a broader spectrum of information, allowing us to perceive and interpret our environment in multi-layered ways. They deepen our understanding of the intricate connections between our body, mind, and the world we inhabit. By attuning ourselves to these additional senses, we expand our capacity for awareness and engage in a richer experience of life.

Embracing the existence of these diverse senses, we open ourselves to a world of possibilities. Our perception is no longer confined to the limitations of the five senses but extends into realms that were once unexplored. This expansion invites us to cultivate a heightened sense of curiosity and appreciation for the complex sensations that shape our existence.

Stress

This is probably the most important topic in this entire book. So if you don't take anything else away from this please take this to heart. The stress hormones that are emitted through our body when the sympathetic nervous system gets turned ON are designed to do their job and then leave through our adrenal system. When they are processed through our body immediately after the danger, they are working perfectly as designed. Unfortunately our bodies have not evolved fast enough to keep up with our society and world.

When the switch is left ON we are actually holding on to the stress hormones. As a practitioner of the Emotion Code and Body Coding™ I am able to release trapped emotions from all parts of a body by speaking energetically through the unconscious mind. This healing modality was created by Dr. Bradley Nelson, who began as a chiropractor and then realized that the body was communicating back in many ways.

The practice has resulted in miraculous healings for my clients, and for so many other practitioners' clients around the world. Trapped emotions are the results of unprocessed emotions. When we suppress our emotions or do not fully process them, they get trapped in different parts of our body. Each trapped emotion is from a different time, space or event. I have come to believe that the trapped emotions are trapped hormones and chemicals. This is what creates emotions.

If those trapped chemicals from stress hormones are left stuck in our body, they create inflammation – which is the root cause of almost every single disease. Inflammation can affect our gut, our brain and our heart. It can affect every area and aspect of our lives.

Many years ago, I was diagnosed with fibromyalgia. This is a disease that affects the entire body in many ways. For me the worst part was the inflammation of my nerves. I felt like I was being eaten alive by fire ants. After doing Body Coding™ on myself I was able to alleviate this pain all together.

Author's note: There are many ways to control and reduce stress. We will discuss this in later chapters. But, I want to speak directly to you now. Our society has created stress as a badge of honor. Like we put in our time and hard work and earned it. This is coming from outside of ourselves - and not from our best inner-self and interests.

Healing Potential

There are many consequences as a result of trapped emotions. Unprocessed emotional experiences find their home in different parts of our bodies. Each trapped emotion condenses the essence of a different moment, space, or event that has imprinted itself upon us. As a practitioner of the Emotion Code and Body Code™, I have witnessed the transformative power of releasing these trapped emotions, allowing for profound healing and restoration.

Trapped emotions can be understood as captured hormones and chemicals within our body. Emotions are intricately woven from these very substances. When stress hormones remain trapped within our system for prolonged periods, inflammation can arise—the root cause of numerous diseases and ailments that aflict us. The far-reaching effects of inflammation can impact crucial areas such as our gut, brain, heart, and virtually every aspect of our lives.

Going back to my personal experience with fibromyalgia, before the diagnosis and the application of the Body Code™ for my own healing, even the gentlest touch was extremely painful. When I look back it becomes evident that stress, trapped emotions, and their ensuing inflammation wreaked havoc on me. Just like they do to many individuals worldwide.

This prompts us to question the pervasive influence of stress in our lives, challenging the societal construct that glorifies stress as a "mark of distinction," one we have supposedly earned. These external pressures often disconnect us from our authentic selves and personal interests, leading us further away from our inner well-being.

Fortunately, there are numerous ways to control and reduce stress. It is crucial to recognize that stress, in its current manifestation, is a creation of our society, spread as a symbol of accomplishment. Yet, the true path to fulfillment lies within our soul, rooted in our best selves. We find this fulfillment by nurturing our inner interests, and aligning with our authentic desires. By unraveling the complex web of stress and acknowledging its profound impact, we empower ourselves to embark on a transformative journey toward self-discovery, holistic well-being, and the realization of our greatest potential.

As mentioned earlier, the parasympathetic nervous system is designed to keep us in homeostasis (the state in which our body works to return back to every time it gets out of balance.) For example, if your blood pressure is too high, your parasympathetic nervous system reduces it back to normal; and your body temperature, hormonal levels, and various physiological processes are all designed to stay in a set range of normal. By regulating these vital elements within a set range of normalcy, our body ensures that it remains in a state of balance and well-being. When we go out of balance either way, our system works diligently to bring it back and to restore the equilibrium, returning it to its optimal functioning.

Author's Note: It's fascinating how our body tries to keep us regulated. When we experience too much pain, our body sometimes counteracts and makes us laugh. Have you ever been so mad and got even madder because you couldn't stop a smile from coming to your face? Or been at a funeral and so grief stricken that you laughed out loud? Maybe you saw the most beautiful baby and just wanted to squeeze them up. That is our body trying to regulate and keep us from going too far to one extreme. The pendulum is at work everywhere - including our bodies.

The energy in our universe is in constant motion; there is absolutely no static placement for energy. That means it moves one way and then another. Our bodies are energy which is in motion all the time. Alignment is integrity, and integrity means we are whole and complete. When our heart, mind, gut, body and soul are aligned, and our body is aligned with the energy of our world, we are in a state of pure potential.

When we are out of alignment our body is doing its best with feelings, emotions, sensations, thoughts, and our intuition telling us we are going off track. The goal of this book is to give you enough information so that you can become aware. This will enable you to make conscious decisions about your alignment and how you are going to deal with it. After reading this book you will have all the knowledge you need to get your body, mind, soul and life into alignment.

Author's Note: I will caution you, though, knowledge is not enough. Knowledge without implementation is useless, and it is very difficult to implement all of this information alone. Action, support and guidance are a must. Throughout my life I have tried and failed many times. But when I started allowing myself to hire coaches, and having them work with me personally and directly, I started unlearning "my crap." All of the limiting beliefs and patterns that were holding me back and keeping me out of alignment started melting away. That's when my life started changing, and I witnessed firsthand miraculous results. Are you ready to begin the lifelong process of seeking pure alignment?

By delving into the pages of this book, you will acquire the necessary knowledge to embark on your own alignment journey. Just make sure to approach this knowledge with the intention of implementing it in your life. Through conscious action, supported by the guidance of mentors, coaches, or like-minded individuals, you can forge a path towards lasting alignment, and unlock the infinite potential that lies within you.

The groundwork for liberation has been laid. You have been given the facts and the unfolding process from where we started to present. This next section titled UNIVERSAL LAWS is designed to briefly explain the laws we're all working with so that when we get to the empowerment part of this book, you will understand and have knowledge and not have to go on blind faith. Albert Einstein put everything in perspective when he said, "I do not believe in the God of theology who rewards good and punishes evil. My God created laws that take care of that. His universe is not ruled by wishful thinking, but by immutable laws."

Universal Laws

1. Law of Energy

The Law of Energy states that energy cannot be created nor can it be destroyed. Energy cannot be transmuted or transformed.

2. Law of Oneness

We live in a universe where everything is energy. Because energy serves as the binding force, an intricate web of connections forms. This harmonizes all elements into a singular entity. How can divisions be conceived when the core essence itself unites everything into a seamless whole?

3. Law of Vibration

The Law of Vibration states that all energy is vibrating at all times. The only difference is the frequency of vibration. How fast or how slow the vibrations are what make things different. Just like a radio wave vibrates, you can only pick up your favorite channel if you are on the right frequency.

4. Law of Correspondence

The Law of Correspondence states that there is a direct correlation between what is happening on the inside compared to what is happening on the outside of us. Everything has a correlation. If you want to know what is happening inside of you, look at the correlation of the outside of your life. And if you want to know why things on the outside of life are going the way they are, look at your life from within.

5. Law of Attraction

The Law of Attraction states that everything that is vibrating on the same frequency is attracted to itself. Everything vibrates at a frequency, so in order to attract anything, your thoughts, feelings and actions need to be on the same frequency of your desire.

6. Law of Action

The Law of Action is part of the creation equation. Everything begins as a thought. Those thoughts create feelings. If it ends there and there is no action, then there is no creation or attraction. But it cannot be just any action. Forced action will repel it because its vibration is low compared to the vibration of your desires. You must be inspired to take action fueled with positive emotions and confident thoughts.

7. Law of Cause and Effect

The Law of Cause and Effect was part of Newton's discoveries. Wherever there is action, there is a cause followed by an effect. There is a direct correlation between the two, and it must happen.

8. Law of Compensation

The Law of Compensation states that you will be equally compensated for all your energy and contributions. Sometimes people associate this law with karma. The saying what comes around goes around is true. When thinking about desires, it means the amount of effort and energy you put in MUST be compensated equally.

9. Law of Relativity

The Law of Relativity means that there are no absolutes. Everything is relative to something else. Your thoughts, feelings and actions are relative to your own personal experiences. You can only understand something when it is relative to something else.

10. Law of Polarity

The Law of Polarity is my favorite. Everything has a polar opposite. For every up there is a down; for every light there is darkness. That means if you don't like something, go the opposite way. I will definitely be diving into this more because this is really where your power is when it comes to the influence of choice and decision.

11. Law of Rhythm

The Law of Rhythm states that everything is cyclical, and that everything is changing. Just like the seasons, tides, even your sleep cycle. Many people throughout history have stated, "This too shall pass." It is the perfect quote for remembering this law.

12. Law of Gender

The Law of Gender means that for creation everything has a masculine and feminine. There is no one or the other. Plants can sometimes have both, but they both must exist.

Law of Timing

This is the law that many people have a problem with. We live in an immediate gratification world – especially since the internet came along. But everything has a gestation period, an amount of time needed in order to be created. Once a kernel is planted in the soil, it needs time to turn into a corn stalk. Once a baby is conceived, it has to go through an entire process before it can sustain life outside the womb. Rushing the timing of anything, or getting frustrated because something isn't happening when you expected it, is the greatest reason for creations not coming to fruition.

"You've always had the power my dear; you just had to learn it for yourself"
– Glinda the Good Witch, *The Wizard of Oz*

From the 1939 American classic movie by MGM, based on Frank Baum's book

CHAPTER 3

Shattering Illusions

Every illusion is a story. It's the story that matches your belief. You now know you can change your belief, and this changes your story. Tough love here – our stories give us rewards. We are either empowered or disempowered by our stories. It is only through true self-reflection that you get to decide if the story is worth the reward. What kind of stories do you really want to give energy to? Think about the stories in your own life which seem to have had a negative outcome. You might be saying, "I would never pick that. It's not what I wanted." But if that's what you have received, then on some level that is the story that was playing inside. Only you can change your stories – which in turn changes your outcome. Every single illusion can be debated.

Let's look at an example: **I can't lose weight.** I have tried everything and it didn't work. What's the reward of this story? You get to eat whatever you want, whenever you want. What is the punishment of this story? You are not at a healthy weight. Your body and lifestyle are being affected. Your prosperity, peace, and passion are being negatively affected because of the laws of correspondence, compensation, cause and effect.

Now that you have looked at both sides of your story, you HAVE NO CHOICE but to make a decision. This is something that most people are not aware of. Once you know something, you can't unknow it. Once you know the reward and punishment of your story, you have no choice but to make a choice. And don't be fooled, no choice – IS A CHOICE. The Law of Cause and Effect is at play here. You are looking at your effects, now you get to choose the causes to make a different effect. Your power is in your CHOICE AND YOUR DECISION.

We often come up with various excuses, which are actually just illusions, to rationalize why we can't pursue our goals or desires. I've heard every excuse there is. Many of them I have made for myself.

Here are some of the most common ones:

1. Age – I'm too old/young to begin something new.
2. Lack of Time – there's not enough time to work, take care of my family...
3. Lack of Resources – I don't have enough money, the right tools, support...
4. Fear of Failing – I'm afraid of failing so I'm not going to start...
5. Comfort Zone – This is just how I am...
6. Past Failures – I've failed too many other times to start again.
7. Fear of Succeeding – I'm afraid of the changes and responsibilities that come with...
8. Negative Self-Image – I don't believe I have what it takes to...
9. External Circumstances – The economy is bad, the location is bad...
10. Procrastination – I will do this *(**fill in the blank with any task or responsibility**)* first before I start on my real desires and goals.
11. Perfectionism – everything needs to be perfect before I start or people won't like what I'm offering.
12. Health Issues – I'm not healthy enough to start...
13. Busy Schedule – I have way too many other things that I need to do so I really can't...
14. Comparison to Others – I'm not good enough at what I want to do if I compare myself to...
15. Lack of Skills – I don't have the knowledge or skills necessary to...

It's important to recognize these excuses and challenge them. While there might be real obstacles, many excuses can be addressed with planning, determination, and a shift in your mindset. Taking responsibility for your own actions and choices is the first step to overcoming these roadblocks and working towards your personal goals.

Shattering your illusions can be painful work, and I do not recommend doing the work alone. It is important when you are working through your beliefs to have someone guide you through the process and be there for you. Get the best coach or mentor you can find. Get someone you trust and respect and then let them help you.

Now let's shatter some of these illusions.

Illusion #1 It's Too Late for Me Because . . .

- 40 – Toni Morrison wrote first novel. Won Pulitzer Prize at 56 and Nobel Peace Prize at 62
- 40 – Vera Wang entered the fashion industry
- 41 – Eric Yuan founded Zoom and 8 years later became a billionaire
- 41 – Martha Stewart published first cookbook
- 43 – Samuel L. Jackson won award for Jungle Fever after years of acting
- 44 – Sam Walton started first Walmart
- 40's – Henry Ford founded Ford Motor Company
- 40's – Stan Lee created The Fantastic Four, Spiderman, Black Panther, X- Men
- 40's – Nelson Mandela became an activist, elected President at 76
- 40's – Jeffery Brotman opened first Costco
- 50 – Charles Darwin published *On the Origin of the Species*

- 50 – Julia Child wrote her first cookbook and was inducted into the Culinary Institute Hall of Fame
- 55 – Duncan Hines wrote a cookbook. In his 70's his name was used for products to indicate high quality because of his reputation
- 50's – Leo Goodwin Sr. began insurance company now known as GEICO
- 50's – Ray Kroc founded McDonald's
- 62 – Colonel Sanders founded Kentucky Fried Chicken
- 60's – Laura Ingalls Wilder wrote the series of *Little House books*
- 60's – Grandma Moses began painting. Died at 101 with 1500 pieces of art
- 70's – Peter Roget published *Roget's Thesaurus*

There are many more examples than this, if you're not convinced yet. Do your own digging and you'll find a lot more proof to shatter this illusion.

Illusion #2 I Have So Many Other Responsibilities It Would Be Selfish of Me To . . .

Our society has made taking care of ourselves and living our lives selfish. That was a story created to keep us disempowered. When we give away our power, our energy, and our passions we are not increasing them for someone else. We can't give these things to anyone. All we do is deplete our own energy and hinder our ability to contribute positively to others.

Being selfish is not taking care of yourself. True selfishness is when you become a burden to family or society because you didn't take care of yourself. Selfishness is keeping your gifts, needed by the world, under lock and key, denying others the benefit of your contributions. Even dying with them still unused and unfulfilled.

We lead by example; do you want to show the world that self-sacrifice is a powerful way to live? To paraphrase Napoleon Hill, sin is anything that goes against you. We were born with a purpose and it takes courage and determination to step up to the plate. Society may have beaten you down, but refrain from adopting the narrative of selfishness.

Instead, we have the opportunity to lead by example and show the world that self-care and pursuing our dreams are powerful and necessary aspects of a fulfilling life. We should reject the notion that self-sacrifice is the ideal way to live. Each of us has a purpose, and it takes courage and determination to rise above the societal pressures that may have held us back. Let us not succumb to the false story of selfishness, but instead embrace our true potential and make a positive impact on the world.

Illusion #3 I Don't Have What It Takes to Become . . .

The belief that you are somehow lacking or undeserving is a manifestation of past trauma, pain, and the exhaustion that comes from feeling beaten down, defeated and/or not good enough. Yes, you may have a history of trauma, pain, and exhaustion that has left you feeling incapable moving forward. While I sympathize with your struggle, I cannot endorse your self-perception.

You don't need to navigate your journey in solitude, and you are now aware of all of the underlying physics, history, and universal laws, as well as the importance of a support system. If you don't have what you need in order to become who you truly are – your true genuine self, then GET IT. It is your birthright to be your best self. Start by becoming proactive. Take some sort of action, even if it seems small to begin embracing your true authentic self.

Think about it. What sets you apart? What distinguishes you from the rest of humanity? It's your own unique combination of experiences –

both challenging and triumphant. It's your talents and natural gifts that contribute to your individuality. Whether it's the impact of past traumas or the brilliance of your talents, each piece of your past experiences and understanding makes you the unique person you are, and there is someone out there who could use your help and advice. The person you are best to serve is the person you were six months ago.

Illusion #4 I am Scared. What If I Fail . . .

First of all let's get this straight – your life is not being graded. Your life is not a school assignment. It's a continuous process of development and growth. Because of how the average school system is set up we've all been brainwashed and programmed into believing that we're constantly being graded on our achievements, even years after graduation. "What if I fail? I might get an F!" What if you fail? What's the worst thing that could happen? Most likely there won't be any bloodshed or loss of life, so it's okay. As far as we know, we only have one chance to live life to the fullest. So what in the world are you waiting for?

We were raised in a world of judgment and false information. Growing is a process. You might fail. You might fall. There is absolutely nothing wrong with that because the only way not to fail is not to try. Each "failure" is actually a retraining and rewiring of your brain. It's a new learning curve. Whatever it is – it's okay. Failure is part of life. That is how our brains get wired. That is how we build brain muscle, thinking power, confidence and personal strength.

Be proud of your failures and celebrate them. You are now one step closer to your dream. Remember when we make judgements on ourselves or others when we play God. Trying to dictate the Law of Timing and gestation is not your role. Your role is listening to that little voice inside your head that says, "What if you . . . or wouldn't you like to . . ." and then taking inspired action. If you fall down or fail, get back up and keep trying. You might even be led down a new and more fulfilling path then you ever dreamed possible.

Get the support you need. Get your own personal cheering section, even if it means hiring someone. This is why there are coaches and mentors. This is what they do best. Don't try to do it all by yourself. And don't deny yourself your dreams and aspirations.

Illusion #5 This is Who I Am. I Can't Change . . .

This statement clearly defies the Law of Rhythm. The Law of Rhythm states that everything is always changing. Think of the ebb and flow of the ocean. It's never at rest, and neither are you. Do you know that your DNA is changing all the time? This is the evolution process. Did you know that every seven years every cell in your body is replaced and changed? Did you know that changing your thoughts, beliefs, actions, or your environment *(which are all under your control)* actually changes your DNA and the DNA of those in the next generations which are yet to come? Your DNA is a state of continuous evolution.

Now is a good time to look at energy healing like the Emotion Code or Body Code™. By using this method of healing you can release some of that which is holding you back, and become free to accepting the fact that you might not like change and want to stay in your comfort zone, but you are powerless over it. You cannot make things stay the same, EVER. Your only power comes in deciding what changes you are going to experience. Are they going to be changes that you decided and created, or changes that were imposed on you because of your lack of choice?

Embracing the understanding that change is inevitable empowers you to take charge of your life and all of the transformations that shape it. By aligning your thoughts, beliefs, and actions with the principles contained in the universal laws, and by seeking support and healing where needed, you can embark on a journey of intentional change and fulfillment that leads to an empowered and purposeful life.

Illusion #6 I Have Tried Before and Nothing Has Ever Worked

This illusion is physically not possible according to the laws of the universe. Specifically the Law of gestation. This Law of Timing operates beyond our personal expectations and desires. Timing is a complex interchange of all kinds of different factors, including personal growth, external circumstances, and the alignment of energies. Our ideas, goals and desires require time and nurturing to come to fruition. If you have failed, it's nothing more than a gentle reminder that change and progress don't happen overnight, nor do they ever seem to happen on our personal timeline – although occasionally they do.

It sometimes takes time for things to develop and manifest. Just because something hasn't worked in the past doesn't mean it won't work with continued effort and a longer time frame. Patience and consistent effort are key here.

If you feel you have failed, think of it instead as an opportunity to learn and make adjustments. Remember the encouraging words of Thomas Edison when asked about making the light bulb. "So how many times did you fail?" Edison's answer was, "I never failed. I just learned ten thousand different ways it didn't work." Every attempt we make contributes to the eventual attainment of our success.

Progress can seem slow initially, but it gains momentum as it moves forward. Your past efforts might not have yielded immediate results, but they could have laid the foundation for your future success. Try asking yourself these questions: Am I attempting to follow someone else's approach or make my own way? Am I unintentionally going down the wrong path? Do I need to pay more attention and possibly shift my course? Rather than becoming disheartened, focus on developing your skills and mindset – not on immediate results.

While it may be tempting to compare our progress with that of others, each individual journey is unique. Successes cannot be replicated without considering the full context of every different experience. It is essential to remain open-minded and curious. Explore different approaches, learn from those who have achieved what you aspire to, and adjust your actions accordingly. Remember, what works for one person may not work the same way for another. Be willing to experiment, adapt, and persist in your pursuit of growth and transformation. Seek guidance from individuals, who have succeeded in their own journeys; by doing this you increase your chances of achieving your desired outcome. Trust in the process of change; honor the Law of Timing and gestation. Remain committed to your personal growth and development.

Illusion #7 I Don't Like Risk and Change

Let me challenge you here. If there were a million dollars across the street, would you risk crossing the road with cars and traffic surrounding you? How would your life change with your newfound wealth? If you're afraid of the risk that sometimes comes with success, is it really just a lack of trust in yourself? Your strategies? Your resources? Ask yourself what it is needed and GET IT.

I understand that risk and change can be uncomfortable and unsettling for many people. It's natural to feel apprehensive about stepping into the unknown or making significant changes in our lives. But what about that thought-provoking scenario above? What are the potential rewards that outweigh all of the risks and uncertainties?

It's essential to recognize that trust in our abilities can be built and nurtured. Take the time to identify what you need to establish that trust within yourself and your journey. Seek out the necessary knowledge, skills, support, or guidance to equip yourself for the challenges ahead. By doing so, you are not simply taking blind risks; you are consciously working within the boundaries of the universal laws, harnessing the power of intention and alignment. Remember that unlike man's laws which can be manipulated and changed – the universal laws NEVER CHANGE and they cannot be manipulated.

These laws, on the other hand, provide a foundation for understanding the principles governing our reality. When you align your actions and beliefs with these laws, you can trust in their inherent wisdom and guidance. By developing a deeper trust in yourself, your strategies, and the harmonious workings of the universe, you can approach risk and change with a greater sense of confidence and assurance.

While it is normal to feel uncomfortable with risk and change, it is important to challenge yourself and explore the possibilities that lie beyond your comfort zone. Embrace the potential for growth, abundance, and transformation that awaits you when you dare to take calculated risks and embrace change with a mindset rooted in trust.

Illusion #8 I am Nobody and Not Important

There is a purpose for everybody and everything. Our universal laws state that there are no accidents. You and your life were part of the universal cause and effects, you are part of the oneness that is all, which means it is impossible to be a nobody. I understand that you feel defeated, and it's ok to sometimes lie down and rest when you need it. But you are reading this book, which means that at least a small part of you believes that you are important, and you are looking for a way to prove it.

There are many ways. Which one is yours? Which is your part of the puzzle? Who are you? Who do you want to be? What are your gifts? What is your purpose? Just where do you belong? *(I promise we will be discussing this later in the book.)* If you are feeling off track and lost, it doesn't mean you have to stay there. Your journey of self-discovery began when you first opened this book. It's time to find your purpose, your passion, your peace, and your prosperity. Let the laws of the universe make it so. Don't force the laws away from you. Ride them peacefully.

And again, I will reiterate. If you are lost and confused, it is natural. That's how the laws of society were set up. But you were purposefully put in this place and you can purposefully RiseUP and fulfill your destiny.

Illusion #9 If it Were Truly that EASY, Wouldn't Everyone Be Doing It?

No, everybody would not be doing it. Why? The answer lies in a quote attributed to an American motivational speaker and author, Jim Rohn. He said, "Living hard is easy, and living easy is hard." Let me explain. Making difficult choices and putting in effort to overcome challenges can eventually lead to a more fulfilling, successful, and easier lifestyle – while choosing an easier path might actually lead to more difficulties and hardships in the long run. So, you might want to ask yourself these questions, "Do I want it easy now and hard later?" or "Do I want it hard now so that I can have it easy for the rest of my life?" This is your choice and your decision.

And think of this; only about one percent of the population has discovered and embraced their true calling and are living in alignment with their purpose. The remaining ninety-nine percent are living hard. A lot of this can be blamed on the fact of how our society has evolved, and the lack of knowledge and understanding of how to attain our true wants and desires not being passed onto the next generation. Societal conditioning and limiting beliefs have been ingrained in us. It requires a conscious effort to challenge and overcome these obstacles. You have the power to choose your own path and decide whether you want to face the challenges now and pave the way for an easier future, or opt for an easier route immediately.

So, let's not wait even one second longer to make a commitment to our dreams. This is your time. Easy is not a requirement for fulfillment. Easy is only accomplished after the hard work of Unlearning the Crap that has been instilled for millennia. Ultimately, the choice is yours to make. It's important to recognize that pursuing your purpose and finding fulfillment may not be effortless, but it is a worthwhile and transformative journey. Are you ready to embrace personal growth and create a life that aligns with your true self to experience long-term ease and fulfillment?

Illusion #10 Ok, I'll Get My Ducks in a Row and Then I Will . . .

The saying "I'll get my ducks in a row and then I will . . ." is often used as a humorous way to express the idea of organizing and preparing oneself before taking action. Sorry, but this is just funny. Whoever made up that crazy saying?

Getting all your ducks in a row is like trying to round up ten kittens. It really makes a better meme than an excuse – and that makes it an illusion.

You will never get all your ducks in a row. Just make a DECISION and then Do It!

Kathy Baldwin, Unlearn the Crap about Personal Success and Empowerment

It's really procrastination, and procrastination is correlated with perfectionism. The time will never be perfect and you will never be perfect, because perfection doesn't exist. It is all relative to something or someone else. Do you want to do it or not? That is all that matters.

If you don't feel ready that makes sense. Keep reading this book and I will do my best to get you ready. If this book is not enough and you need more, then reach out to me. I truly want to help you attain your goals. If not me, then no hard feelings; reach out to another coach or mentor you trust will help you. It's time for us to come back to community, to our tribe, to our support system. We were never ever meant to go this journey alone. We were never ever meant to know everything, to do everything or to be everything. That is part of the societal abuse that kept us disempowered. Making us believe that until we are perfect, we're not ready. We were taught once we're perfect we're worthy. This just isn't true. You're worthy! Accept that fact at this moment.

It only happens, when you decide. You have that power right now. Stop procrastinating by overcoming your fear of imperfection.

Perfectionism and procrastination can be detrimental because they often lead to inaction or delay. The truth is that there will never be a perfect time or perfect set of conditions to start. Waiting for everything to be in order only delays your progress and prevents you from taking the necessary steps towards your dreams and aspirations. Break free from the mindset that you have to have it all figured out before beginning. Embrace the journey ahead. Remember, the most important thing is your willingness and commitment to pursue what you truly desire.

> *"The only way to deal with an unfree world is to become so absolutely free that your very existence is an act of rebellion."*
> —Albert Camus

Albert Camus was a French-Algerian philosopher, author, dramatist, and journalist. He was the recipient of the 1957 Nobel Prize in Literature at the age of 44. He was the second-youngest recipient in history.

His works include: *The Stranger, The Plague, The Myth of Sisyphus, The Fall,* and *The Rebel*.

CHAPTER 4

What If I Really Become Successful?

Who will I be?
Will I still be liked?
Can I handle it?
Will I be different?
Can I trust myself?

Have you ever asked yourself these questions? They are all really good questions, but they're also demons hiding in the dark. These demons have been shot straight through our hearts from the gun of guilt and they have filtered into the core of our being. Guilt makes us second guess ourselves. It is also a sign of control to keep you smaller than you are. If you admit that you are truly successful – that is not humble. And if you're not being humble then you are being shameful. This is how many of us have been confused into thinking that being successful is somehow shameful.

Do you know that shame is the lowest vibration or emotion that there is? Do you know that shame is also a manmade emotion? Through generations of storytelling of how people in power have acted badly and manipulated the poor and downtrodden, we've evoked emotions through narratives and characters intentionally or unintentionally designed to make us feel bad if we succeed and someone else doesn't. Many of these stories make us believe that if we gain someone else loses. This concept in itself creates shame. Shame's purpose is to control us by using someone else's opinion and definition of right and wrong. It should never have existed, and it's time to banish it.

The thing about limitations is that we usually only associate them with the negative. The more sinister and powerful ones are actually the positive limitations, because they fool our brain into thinking we are doing what is best for us and everyone else.

Positive limitations are self-sacrificing. We want to be liked and accepted. These limitations trick us into believing we're doing what is right, but in truth, these limitations are lies our brain is feeding us. We have already discussed the parts of the brain, and how together they process information. We have already discussed the disempowering social narrative that we believe is truth. Positive limitations are the accumulation of all of that. Let me explain.

Fear is a signal that you need to pay attention to what is happening. It doesn't necessarily mean that it is wrong, that you should retreat, or that something bad is happening. But this is the definition we have been taught. Fear means that you are encroaching on something for which your unconscious brain does not have a program. That means you will be going without the safety net of all the preprogrammed responses. This can be a good thing because rinse and repeat just gives you more of the same.

Take a piece of paper and, in the center of the paper, write down everything you have currently in your life, relationships, health, wealth, lifestyle, possessions etc. Write it all down – everything you value that you already have. Now draw a circle around those items.

Next on the outside of the circle write down everything that you do not have but that you want. All of your dreams, all of those experiences, all the possessions, the wealth, the health, the relationships. Everything.

Everything on the inside of that circle is IN your comfort zone. You have it. There is no stress, there is no unknown, it is there already for you.

Everything outside of that circle is all unknown. It hasn't been accessed, received, experienced or attained yet. The unknown creates stress for the unconscious mind, and that shows up as fear. There is a physiological translation to that response and we feel it in our bodies.

The line of the circle is our comfort zone. Everything you want is on the outside of your comfort zone. I want you to think of something that you wanted for a long time. When you were about to get it, did it not scare, exhilarate and terrify you all at the same time?

Let me give an example. For those of you who have children, when you were wanting children, there was a desire. When you were expecting there was excitement, but at some point, usually close to the birth, you probably got terrified thinking you weren't ready. You didn't know what to do because you hadn't experienced it yet. What if you failed? What if you dropped the baby? What if . . . what if . . . what if . . .

The same thing happens with every new major, or even every new minor, thing in our lives. Just as we are on the threshold, our subconscious mind sends all sorts of warnings saying, "Watch out! I can't protect you here! This is unknown to me." This all happens in a language that is completely foreign and unknown to us. So we don't realize what's going on.

But what if you knew and understood the language? What if you could speak to your subconscious mind like you would to a child who was scared of a new event? What would you say to a toddler afraid to jump into a pool? You would probably say something like, "Don't worry, I got you. I won't let you go under." Or how about a teenager getting ready for college. You might say something like, "It's all planned for you to excel. You'll be studying what you love. I know this part of the process is uncomfortable, but you will see in hindsight that it was all good. Until then, you have to trust that together we have the skills, the knowledge and ability to handle anything that we come up against."

How would that comfort zone line feel to you then? It makes me feel a little braver just typing it.

There is another part of this fear of success. It comes in the form of how you will be perceived by the outside world. That's when your identity takes a hit. Your identity changes every single time you grow. Your identity changed when you went from a baby to a toddler. From a teenager to an adult. It changed when you went from a student to having a career. Maybe you even went from a career to a business owner. It changed when you went from single to married, from married to divorced or widowed. Life is about transitions and change, and each of those changes comes with an identity change.

The hard truth about this is, you will continue to change and evolve and so will all the people in your life. The Law of Rhythm shows us that everything is in constant motion and in cycles. People will come and go in your life and you cannot ever control or hold things the same. Trying to do that is insanity and it will never work.

Marianne Williamson says it like this, Our deepest fear is not that we are inadequate. Our deepest fear is that we are powerful beyond measure." Our power is fierce and awesome. We have been trained to be afraid of that kind of power rather than learning how to harness it. In this book of Unlearn the Crap, one of the biggest things I want you to realize is:

- **You have the power.**
- **You are the power.**

You are created from and with the power.

You cannot escape it. And it is wonderful and miraculous. And so are you!

We will be discussing identity in the next chapter, but I want you to know that when you choose and you decide what your identity is, what you are creating, what direction you are heading in, and you know and accept yourself in all your glory, then fear is a sign you are on the right track. It should be celebrated. If you are not fearful, you are stagnant.

And like a river that is stagnant, it becomes toxic and poisonous. We must remain in flow. That is the purpose of life.

Let's address this fear of change that comes up when we hit the place of positive limitations. Again, if you look at the root cause of this, you will see that it is a belief that has been instilled in you. You were not afraid of learning to walk, even though you fell so many times. You were not afraid of learning to talk, even though you made more mistakes in the sounds and words than you can count. We were designed for growth. We were built in an ever- expanding universe, and we are ever-expanding beings.

This is why you need to be clear with your choices, decisions, and expectations. In my life I have found the greatest source of pain and disappointments came from expectations. When we put limitations or expectations on how things "should" be, they never ever happen that way. Our minds need to open up to all of the different possibilities instead of expecting certain outcomes. Expectations give us a sense of control, but possibilities open us up to faith in the unknown and the miraculous.

It becomes obviously necessary to embrace discomfort. Not as a form of punishment, but because you now understand that it is a survival mechanism. It is part of our brain's programming and functions because of our society and history. Your discomfort is a glorious sign of growth, expansion, and possibilities.

Let me share a personal story with you. One of my favorite questions to ask people when I meet them is about their favorite meal. Where it was, what it was, and what made it so special. The answers always tell me so much about the person. Let me share with you my favorite meal experience.

I was in Amsterdam and taken out for dinner at a restaurant called the 5 Flies. It was a series of old houses that had been opened up to each other to be a stone building with so much history and emotions built right into the walls. These houses were owned by the Fly family, and each member had their own house. You could feel it.

When it came time to order, you could either order off the menu or you could choose the chef's choice. When you chose the chef's choice you could only choose how many courses you wanted. That was it. The rest was out of your control. Everyone that I was with chose off the menu but I took the chef's choice. Every single plate was an adventure; it was a gift. I had no idea what was coming but it was pure joyful pleasure. Every bite tasted better because I had zero expectations or anything to compare it to. It was a blissful moment in time.

How do you want to live your life? Do you want to live off a limited menu that comes with connections to past experiences, emotions, and expectations, or do you want to live limitlessly, joyfully open to whatever comes next, knowing that each moment will be more glorious than the previous?

Discomfort comes when we want to control and enforce, but what if you were to experience and create instead?

It all comes down to our choices. What we want from our life. I know this may be a new way of looking at your life and what you can create. Are you afraid of the wrapped gift? Or do you anticipate how wonderful it will be as you open it?

I want to address the life you were born into and look at it from a bird's eye view. When you were born, the first thing that you were identified by was your genitals. Are you a boy or a girl? Imagine if when you were born the first thing that happened was that the people who surrounded you looked deep into your eyes and saw the soul that just arrived, regardless of the package it arrived in.

That social identity then moved on to how you were clothed, what toys you were expected to play with and identify with. You were raised in a box of expectations based on the outside of you.

Those gender stereotypes are crippling to individuality and self-acceptance, especially when the roles are extreme. Your ability to express yourself, your emotions, and your thoughts was decided based on what body parts were found between your legs.

What about your heart? And your heart energy? What emotions were you vibrating with? What about your thoughts, your natural inclinations? Your dreams?

What if your natural self went against what the societal norms said you were "supposed" to be or do or feel or love? Do you feel the discord? Do you understand the pain in misalignment internally based on someone or something else telling you what you "should" be, do, or feel?

How do those expectations show up in your life and career path? Were you guided by your internal natural self or by societal norms, or even worse by the evolution of life events?

There is a question that I hear people ask all the time, "If you could go back, what career would you have chosen? Would it be different from where you found yourself?" Most people say yes. It's only with time and space that they actually began to know themselves.

Author's note: I just saw a video on the correct way to stir your tea: back and forth - not round and round. Seriously??? These outside expectations we have been brought up in can be crazy. Imagine being deemed unacceptable because of the direction you stir your tea! It's so superfluous and irrelevant, but it has been reasoned important by outside influences. It's truly scary to me how our have been suffocated by expectations.

Let's continue down the road of societal expectations based on age, beauty, or body size and shape. I spent most of my life in sales training and management, and every year there were trade shows for the newest colors, models, designs etc. It was all designed to keep a perpetual market need for acceptance of what was in and what was out, all for profit.

If you look at history, the same can be said about our age, beauty, and body size. In the 60's bone thin was considered the "in" look. Historically old age was an earned esteem of wisdom, then it changed and old age made you irrelevant depending on the circumstances. In our modern age beauty is seen and judged by what we see on the outside: skin color, makeup, hair design, body size; it's all about physical attributes that are judged by an outside source.

Add to that the social expectations on marriage, family size, sexual attraction, mental health, racial and ethnic stereotypes, religions and beliefs, comparisons, conformity. All of it judged by where you live because each geographic location has different rules and expectations.

When you really stop and look at it – it's crazy. As you can plainly see, one of the greatest self-sabotaging traits comes from people-pleasing. The desire to meet expectations and be found acceptable by others.

Think for a second about the three most important words everyone wants to hear; most people would say they are: I love you. As wonderful as those are to hear, coming from someone who you love, they are from the outside of you. Those three words have been sought after for millennia. These three beautiful little words have held so much power that people have killed for them. Have you ever thought about the power we give the words "I love you"? They basically mean if someone says they love you – now you are deemed acceptable.

What if the three most important words were: Passion, Purpose and Peace? These are internal words. They can only be found by going inside your soul, the piece of who you truly are. Doing this brings those traits out into the world and expands not only yourself, but the world itself.

Author's note: The reason I am so compelled to write this book and bring my courses and knowledge into the world is that I TRULY believe it is time to UNLEARN THE CRAP!!! All of it - the control and disempowerment. None of that really matters.

We started this chapter on the what if's… all of the what if's based on societal and external norms and expectations. I am going to take what if to a whole new level. Stay with me on this – it may rufle the feathers of what you have been taught.

Here's what we know to be true according to science:

- Energy is the root of everything, and it takes charged energy in order to create.
- We live in an electromagnetic, biomechanical world – in electromagnetic, biomechanical physical bodies.
- Energy vibrates at different frequencies and those frequencies can be measured.
- The highest vibrating frequency is love and God Consciousness.

Now for the *What Ifs*:

- What if all of the religions were based on people vibrating at the highest frequencies?
- What if we could all attain the same vibrational frequencies as those living in pure love and pure God Consciousness frequency?
- Every religion tells us that through faith, we can achieve anything. What if faith is the way to higher frequencies?
- What if we believed and trusted and let go of trying to control and being controlled?
- What if one was esoteric and the other was electromagnetic? The same thing expressed differently?

In my over 40 years of study, I have come to understand that everyone is saying the same thing, just from different perspectives and angles. Science, religion, quantum physics, medicine, personal development, biology. Everyone is saying the same thing.

We have the power. We are the power. We are "of" the power. There is no separation.

This is why outside influences, norms, and expectations have been so strongly imposed on us. If we really knew and accepted that we are equal, the same, connected, and interconnected then where do control, hate, and anger live? They have no home if we don't let them in, and therefore they must die. If those die within us then by the Law of Polarity we all naturally step into: Love, Acceptance, Joy, and Inclusion.

Think of soldiers walking in unison. If everyone is in step and paying attention to the drummer and the drill sergeant, they are easily controlled. It would be much harder to control them if they were all walking to the beat of their own drum. Their own destination, their own timeline. When we are consolidated, conformed, and united as one, it's easy for someone or something else to lead that harnessed power.

Think about these popular sayings: Fall in line. Keep your head in the game. Keep your nose to the grindstone. Roll up your sleeves and get to work. The road to success is paved with hard work and determination. Don't wait for an opportunity – create it. Stop daydreaming and get back to work.

All of these sayings are in the physical, and controllable by outside forces. What is not controllable is our thoughts, our vibrations, our dreams, our visions, our emotions. Those are where the power lies. Keeping us disconnected from that power, allows us to be controllable and managed. Victor Frankl was in a Nazi prison camp during WWII. He is known for saying, "The one thing they couldn't control was my mind." This reflects Frankl's belief that even though he had lost control over many aspects of his life while in the concentration camp, he retained the ability to choose his attitude and mental outlook.

We all have the right to knowledge, but we also have the responsibility for self-empowerment and self-direction.

It's time to be consciously aware of our interconnection, our oneness, our entanglement, and our universal power. Understand how raising up all of our vibrations changes the entire world's experience. Know that we can't do anything but love and accept and give and take equally when living in line with the universal laws. This is when we will know and experience our true inner power.

What if...

- You knew you had the power?
- You knew how to access and utilize it?
- You and everyone else were connected to the same high vibrating field of energy?
- You were guided from internal guidance and inspiration rather than external force?
- You released the physical energy and pain that has disconnected you from yourself?
- You brought your gifts to the world and became the greatest version of yourself?
- Everyone else did the same?

Think about these *What Ifs* and then take some time to jot down your thoughts and answers to these questions:

What would be different?

_____

_____

_____

_____

How would you and your world change?

_____

_____

_____

_____

How would our society change?

_____

_____

_____

_____

What could you accomplish?

_____

_____

_____

_____

What would be impossible?

_____

_____

_____

Who would you be?

_____

_____

_____

_____

When embarking on a journey of self-discovery and personal growth, it's natural to have questions and concerns about who you will become, how others will perceive you, whether you can handle the changes, and whether you can trust yourself. These questions often stem from the internalized beliefs and judgments that have been imposed on us by society.

Remember, there are no mistakes in this world. And that includes you – you are not a mistake. Your authentic, true self is meant to shine. You are meant to lead, RiseUP and make a positive difference in the world.

What truly matters is not how the world defines you, but rather the impact you can make by Rising Up and bringing others with you. There will always be individuals who try to bring you down to their level, but imagine the difference you could make by empowering them to RiseUP alongside you. By embracing your true authentic self on your journey of self-discovery you inspire and uplift not only yourself – but also those around you.

"Be vulnerable. Let yourself be deeply seen, love with your whole heart, practice gratitude, joy... be able to say 'I am thankful to feel this vulnerable because it means I am alive.' And believe I am enough.
You are worthy of love and belonging."
—Brené Brown

Brené Brown is an American professor, author, and podcast host. Brown is known for her work on shame, vulnerability, and leadership, and for her widely viewed TEDx talk in 2010. She has written six number-one *New York Times* bestselling books and hosted two podcasts on Spotify.

CHAPTER 5

How Do I Discover Who I Am When I Feel So Lost?

I did not grow up with the understanding that I could deliberately choose what my values, beliefs, vision, purpose, and even personal boundaries were, and how they would affect me and impact my life. I knew what they were for business and applied them easily, but personally they were never on my radar . . . until I had a nervous breakdown.

My nervous breakdown took everything away from me, literally. I lost EVERYTHING! Finances. Relationships. My home. My sense of security. But the worst thing I lost – was me. I didn't know who I was or how to cope. I made horrible mistakes. I knew better, so that made it even worse when I did them anyway. This all led me to a place where I no longer trusted myself.

I have gone through a lot; more than most people could ever imagine, but that time was truly the scariest part of my life, and that is saying a lot! But it was also the greatest gift I ever had.

I did get an insight into the power of our brain and being out of alignment with self when this happened. I experienced a profound sense of relief, and I realized that my unconscious mind had been pulling me down every time I pushed myself up. When I lost everything, I was fully aligned with my unconscious mind, and it felt at peace. I didn't feel at peace, but my brain did. What a horrible way to live, constantly fighting an internal battle with yourself.

I was left with absolutely nothing. There was nothing to save. There was nothing to fight for. There was nothing to distract me. All I had was me.

And if I didn't have a clear understanding of my own identity, I realized it was time for me to start utilizing the wisdom I had been gaining from various experts for the last forty years, and recreate my life. It was time to be the person I had been longing to be. It was time to align myself internally and externally. It was time to recreate me.

While I had been doing the busy work of working on only external factors, I kept being pulled back down. It was time to clean house and do the hard work of creating and aligning myself with my highest version of myself.

And I did. For the next two years I worked on the basics, and I set out to define who I was going to be in the future. Because it was painfully obvious that who I was in the past did not work!

Author's Note: I highly recommend you learn from my mistakes and begin your self-discovery journey now. I don't want another person to lose themselves and have a breakdown. There are easier and gentler ways to finding your true self - especially if you have someone by your side to guide you.

I had the Big Me inside the Broken Me guiding me. It was rough. It was hard. There were times I lay on the floor curled in a ball sobbing like a wounded animal, sounds I had never heard coming out of me before.

Today is the first day of the rest of your life and where you are now is the perfect place to begin.

Take the necessary time to really understand the principles and convictions we have already discussed, and those that you're about to read below. Instead of being who you are based on what life threw at you, begin consciously designing your life and yourself.

If you need someone who knows the road because they have travelled it, I'm right here; you can reach out to me. My coaching clients appreciate that my approach isn't from a rigid program or organization; it's rooted in real life experience. I guide from real life experience and scientifically supported methods that combine all the latest mind, brain, and body healing. I'm offering my services to support you if you need them.

Values

What ARE values?

Values are the guiding principles that shape our beliefs, decisions, and actions. They are the deeply held convictions that reflect what we consider important and meaningful in life. Our values serve as a compass, influencing our behaviors, priorities, and overall sense of purpose.

At their core, values represent the essence of who we are and what we stand for. They provide a framework for making choices, and help us navigate the complexities of life. Our values shape our relationships, career paths, and personal growth. They contribute to our overall well-being and fulfillment.

Values are not static; they evolve and adapt as we gain new experiences and insights. They can be influenced by our upbringing, culture, and personal aspirations. Identifying our values allows us to align our actions with what truly matters to us, fostering a sense of authenticity and congruence in our lives.

Why should I care and put the effort into it? Nobody I know ever has.

Values are like the bone structure of our lives. They are our foundation and structure. If we try to live our lives based on our dreams and aspirations, without ensuring that the foundation is strong enough to support it, we are creating our own disaster.

Just like renovating a house, the first thing that is done is to ensure that the structure and foundation are in integrity and aligned with the vision of the design. This is why I recommend starting here. You can choose who you are, who you want to be, today and in the future. You are in fact choosing to design yourself, knowing that your life changes the minute you change your thoughts, feelings, and actions.

Living in accordance with our values brings numerous benefits. It enhances our self-awareness and self-confidence, when we are grounded in our beliefs and principles; providing a sense of clarity and purpose, helping us set meaningful goals and make decisions that align with our authentic selves.

When our actions are in harmony with our values, we experience a greater sense of fulfillment, inner peace, and integrity. Conversely, when our actions contradict our values, we may feel a sense of dissonance and dissatisfaction. When you have not done the exercise of seeing what values you currently have, and if they are in alignment with your authentic self, the stress and disconnect can be devastating.

Values also play a vital role in your relationships. Shared values create a sense of connection and understanding, while conflicting values can lead to misunderstandings and conflict. By recognizing and respecting the values of others, we foster empathy, collaboration, and harmonious interactions.

To lead a meaningful and purposeful life, it is crucial to identify and honor our values. By consciously aligning our choices and actions with our core values, we empower ourselves to live authentically and create a positive impact on the world around us. Values make decisions and choices so much easier to make; they find a place where you are a hard NO or a strong YES and everything else falls in the middle.

Now that you know how important your values are, make a list of all of them that you hold dear. Go deep, don't just stay on the surface because on the surface is only your mind, which has already been programmed.

You want to go deep within, to your heart and your gut – that is where the real you speaks. If you need inspiration, go to the internet and you will find exhaustive lists of values. Choose your most important, moderately importance, and least important as a good place to start.

CAUTION STOP: Do not keep reading until after you do this exercise, otherwise nothing further will be of value to you. *Unless you have chosen to read through once and then come back to do the work, which is how some of my clients prefer it.*

Personally, I like to dive in, without knowing the next step so I am open to being led by divine intelligence and my highest inner self. Knowing the step ahead of time gives room for the egoic, programmed, unconscious mind to kick in and take over, again.

List the **Top Ten Values** you hold most important here:

1. _____

2. _____

3. _____

4. _____

5. _____

6. _____

7. _____

8. _____

9. _____

10. _____

Beliefs

I have already shown you how your current beliefs are formed. They are programs that come from a stimulus that is attached to an emotion and an outcome. If you survive that, then your subconscious mind believes it worked and will repeat the pattern every subsequent time, until it becomes a belief and then a habit.

When you are looking at your beliefs, I want you to look at them from the list of values you just wrote. Look at them from the place of the person you are choosing to design.

What beliefs would that person have in order to uphold those values? What beliefs do you currently hold that contradict the version of yourself that you are creating?

What would that person believe about relationships, about health, wealth, and spirituality? What would that person need to believe to be the person you are designing in every area of your life?

Let me give you an example of how this works. If your decision to value challenge, adventure, autonomy are your true authentic self but you currently carry the belief that family, community and faith are the beliefs you currently carry as your priority, do you see the disconnect? Do you see how you would be pulled internally, probably without even being aware of it?

That is how I want you to work through and create your own beliefs.

Again, do not continue this process until you have completed this exercise. Everything is set up the way I coach my clients, in a sequential order. Building one step at time from the foundation and core of who you are now, up to your best self. If you feel overwhelmed doing this identity work, I encourage you to reach out to someone who can help you through this process. It can be very emotional taking a true look at who you naturally are, who society has formed you to be and where changes will need to take place.

List the **Top Ten Beliefs** you hold most important here:

1. _____

2. _____

3. _____

4. _____

5. _____

6. _____

7. _____

8. _____

9. _____

10. _____

Boundaries

Boundaries. This one blew me away. My upbringing was about how to be perceived in the world, how to function in the world, but that world did not keep up with the ever-changing times.

I never knew that I could actually say, "NO." I never believed that I could set my own boundaries, because I had the belief that everyone else was more important than me. How did I get those beliefs? No one ever said it to me. I was never encouraged to be a doormat or let people walk all over me. No, my parents believed in me and tried to raise me to be the best version of myself. They knew and saw my potential and my intelligence. They always pushed and encouraged me, the best way they knew how, based on how they were raised by parents that did the best they knew how . . . and on and on it goes. Get my point? Socialized values and morals that were adapted to fit the environment of the times and down through the ages went.

Now we know better, and like Maya Angelou says, "When you know better you do better."

Once I knew how beliefs were formed, I applied my business training to run a root cause analysis of my beliefs. As I mentioned earlier, I drew upon every resource I had from all areas of training: business, professional, personal and developmentally. It's a reminder that you never know when skills from unexpected sources will come to your rescue.

I discovered that I held the belief that I did not belong here, and that I needed to provide value to everyone else in order to earn my belonging.

My childhood brain took the knowledge that my parents married because I was on the way – something that's happened all through the ages. That meant that I wasn't planned and I wasn't wanted. As inaccurate as it was – this was a heavy burden to carry, and it shaped my tendency to prioritize others above myself. I always, and I mean always, put everyone else ahead of me, in every area of my life. This predisposition played a key role in my eventual breakdown – but provided a turn of events for which I am now grateful.

The truth was my parents loved each other until they died. They were married for over 44 years and died 7 weeks apart. I was adored and cherished. But when a belief takes hold inside your mind it censors out anything that contradicts the framework, selecting and screening out what it so chooses.

So, if my belief said that I was to put everyone ahead of me because they mattered and I didn't, how would the thought of saying No or creating safe boundaries ever enter my mind?

Do you know what happens when you don't have boundaries? People come into your life and take anything and everything you have, in every and any way. How do I know? Experience.

After being taken advantage of, I would blame myself because I knew better. I was smart, successful, strong, and capable. I could handle anything that was thrown at me. I could do more work than most people. In reality I did more work than most people because of my lack of boundaries and my belief that I had to prove I was worthy. This is really just another form of self-sabotage.

Working harder and more than others, pretending to be superman/superwoman, only pushes people away. Sometimes it makes people feel things about themselves that really aren't important.

Author's note: I have since come to realize that what I say and do is about me, and what you say and do is about you. Our only true power is focusing on yourself and letting others live their own lives for themselves.

When finding your boundaries I want you to look at all the major events of your life, good, bad, and especially ugly. Look at what you had to believe in order for each event to unfold. Ask yourself if you had boundaries? If so, how did you use them? Assess them based on your new list of values and decide whether or not they fit the new you.

Even though the past is over and really doesn't exist anymore, it is important to evaluate the past and future together because you carry stories in your mind about events based on your past experiences. This is why it is important to understand and study the universal laws of relativity and polarity and how they work. These stories in your mind are not tangible, and they are in the past. We are building the *you* that you want to be now and in the future. Taking what happened and applying it to your new vision will make the next steps fall into place. Trust me, I have thought this through, and at the end you will have a major ah-ha moment.

Before moving on take some time now in the space provided to express your thoughts now about your **BOUNDARIES** then and now based on your new list of values:

_____

_____

_____

_____

_____

_____

_____

_____

_____

_____

_____

_____

_____

_____

_____

_____

_____

_____

Ethics & Morals

Ethics and morals are closely related concepts that shape our behaviors and guide our interactions with others. While they are often used interchangeably, there are subtle distinctions between the two.

Ethics refers to a set of principles or standards that define what is considered right or wrong, good or bad, in a particular context or field. It provides a framework for decision-making and guides our conduct in various spheres of life, including personal, professional, and societal realms. Ethical principles are derived from values and often encompass notions of fairness, honesty, respect, and responsibility.

One of our inherent faculties is a built-in sense of justice and ethical discernment. There is an internal compass within you, eagerly providing you with guidance to keep you on the right path. However, the question is, are you listening?

Morals, on the other hand, are individual beliefs and judgments about right and wrong. Morals are influenced by personal values, cultural norms, religious beliefs, and upbringing. They reflect an individual's subjective understanding of what is morally acceptable or unacceptable. Morals can vary from person to person, while ethics tend to be more standardized and commonly accepted within a particular context.

In everyday life, ethics and morals play a significant role in shaping our actions and decisions. They provide an innate moral guide that helps us navigate those ethical dilemmas. They help us make choices that align with our principles. Here are some examples of how ethics and morals apply to our daily lives:

1. **Personal Relationships:** Ethics and morals influence how we treat others, such as being honest, loyal, and respectful in our interactions. They guide us in making decisions that prioritize the well-being and dignity of others, fostering trust and harmony in our relationships.

2. **Professional Conduct:** Ethics govern our behavior in the workplace, ensuring fairness, integrity, and professionalism. They guide us in making ethical decisions when faced with conflicts of interest, maintaining confidentiality, and upholding the ethical standards in our chosen professions.

3. **Social Responsibility:** Ethics extend to our role in society. They encourage us to be responsible citizens, respecting the rights and well-being of others. Ethical considerations may guide us in contributing to social causes, promoting equality, and practicing sustainable behaviors.

4. **Ethical Consumption:** Our ethical values can shape our choices as consumers. This includes considerations such as supporting ethical and sustainable businesses, making informed purchasing decisions, and avoiding products or practices that violate our ethical principles.

5. **Moral Dilemmas:** In everyday life, we may encounter moral dilemmas where our personal morals conflict with ethical principles or societal norms. These situations require thoughtful reflection and ethical decision- making. They help us navigate the complexities and choose the course of action that aligns with our values, while respecting the rights and well- being of others.

You have created your values, designed the beliefs needed in order to live out those values, and you have created boundaries to keep you safe. When you use ethics and morals for decision-making along with your values, beliefs and boundaries for every future event in your life, it's easier to choose what it is that you truly want, and your choices will align with who you really are.

Ethics are right or wrong. Black or white. There is no room for gray areas in ethics. When you're making future decisions or choices, ask yourself,

"What feels like a clear 'yes' or 'no' based on what's right or wrong for me?" Those decisions then become easy. Some choices will still be tough — that's when morals come into play.

Morals are influential when you're dealing with the uncertainties that exist between your definite "yes" or "no." Have there been instances where you've been critical or judged yourself unfairly? Are there moments you wish you could redo? Examine these events and DECIDE how you'll handle similar situations in moving forward.

Do you see the simplicity that comes with selecting the path you desire? When you are in control of the direction you're going? When you establish clear boundaries that define who you are? This is the foundation of your identity. Imagine the inner strength you possess, when you can stand strong and say, "This IS who I am and that is NOT who I am," or acknowledging, "I've evolved and today I choose a different self."

Needs & Wants

Okay, here we go . . . Let's start having fun. When I was a kid I was told, "Kathy, is it a need or a want? If it's a want, it's a No." Why? Who made that rule?

Needs are the rock for our foundation. Needs are what allows you to go into the world with safety and the security of knowing all is well. When you feel your needs are met — nothing will shake your foundation. This is my definition of needs. I want you to explore what your definition is.

Wants are our inner self, directing us to our next step. It's not really the attainment of the want that our inner self is guiding us towards, but it's who we become on the journey. It's who and what we affect when receiving that want.

Have you ever noticed that when people win lotteries, they usually lose it all very soon after? I realized when I lost everything and had to start all over again, it was because what I had clashed with my identity. I wasn't seeing myself for who I truly was. It's important to take the journey and be actively present when achieving your wants. This is where gratitude plays a vital role.

Wants, dreams, and desires are given to us so we grow. Our identity is like a thermostat that is set to a specific degree and it's always trying to get us back to our preset location. If you want to know where your preset temperature is, look around you. Your day to day reality IS your preset location. If you want more, you need to actively work on recalibrating your life and making your wants feel normal.

I was raised to believe that only Santa gave us our wants. That is if we were good little girls and boys. Because remember, he was always watching and always knew if we were behaving or not. Behaving was the requirement to get your wants. And if you were bad, based on "Santa's" judgement, then you got coal. This is a dreadful belief to put in children's heads. What a terrible reinforcement to a person with a negative personal belief. Yes, children need to have consequences, but let's come up with a better way than that. No wonder so many of us feel as though we're not worthy and carry the guilt of not measuring up.

One of the first retreats I attended was with James Arthur Ray from the movie *The Secret*. We did an exercise that taught us how to break boards with our bare hands, while releasing a negative belief that was not serving us. After everyone had completed the exercise, James asked the audience, "What was the belief that you released?"

99% of the audience said, "I am not good enough." Then James told us something even more shocking. He said that at every one of his events the answer is always the same; people truly don't believe they are worthy.

Can you believe most people in this world genuinely believe they are not good enough to receive their wants and desires? Our societal abuse has generations of people feeling like they really don't measure up. This is a form of torment that feels exceptionally cruel, especially when we know that we are capable of so much more. But we're trapped by invisible ropes and unseen bonds that are holding us down.

Author's Note: Yes, I broke the board with my bare hand on the first try. It was such a rush knowing I was capable of doing more than I ever believed about myself.

Now that I have done the work and understand the purpose of needs, I know they are meant to be in our life for a reason. It is not selfish to dream. Dreams are like the carrot that our higher self is using to guide us to where we are meant to be. Our wants should be continuous. Once we receive something we will soon find another want that will make us step out of our comfort zone and grow. We should never catch the carrot because it keeps urging us on. In the grand scheme, it's the journey that truly counts. The journey includes all the obstacles, the relationships, and the meaningful impact and influence we make on the world by becoming who our inner self is guiding us to be.

I once saw an interview with Goldie Hawn. It was interesting how she described marriage. She said, "If we were all financially independent and didn't need a partner to ensure that all of our financial needs were met, then we could truly choose who we wanted to marry." It is in our authentic power, and our authentic knowledge of ourselves that we can truly make any choice for ourselves.

It's time to create your **LIST of NEEDS** now. What do you need for your foundation? What do you need that is a MUST HAVE? You must make sure you first have your foundation covered. Your wants are fun and exciting and so enlightening, but we'll be making your list of WANTS later in the book. Don't forget to put your financial independence as a foundational need. Without your financial needs being independently met, you will never truly be able to set foot into your true power.

_____

_____

_____

_____

_____

_____

_____

_____

_____

_____

_____

_____

_____

_____

_____

_____

Mission

Personal Mission Definition: To inspire and empower individuals to unlock their full potential, cultivate meaningful relationships, and make a positive impact on the world.

A personal mission is a guiding purpose or grand vision providing a sense of direction and meaning to your life. It's your own personal map. It helps you know what you want and what to do. It's your BIG dream. It includes your core values, passions, and aspirations, serving as a compass for decisions making and goal setting. It reflects your unique journey and the contributions you want to make in your personal and professional spaces. Your mission is the impact you want to create in the world.

A well-crafted mission statement reflects clarity, inspiration, and a sense of purpose.

Here is an example of a personal mission statement — which happens to be mine:

Live fully integrated with myself and Universal energy, so that everything I do has meaning and purpose, which makes a difference in the world, because I was Born to be Alive.

It is essential to reflect on your values, passions, and the desired impact you want to make to know what your mission truly is. Take time now to reflect and then create a personal mission statement that resonates with your true authentic self. This guiding framework will provide clarity, motivation, and a sense of fulfillment as you navigate your life's journey.

My Personal Mission Statement

Date _____

_____

_____

_____

_____

_____

_____

_____

_____

_____

_____

_____

_____

_____

_____

_____

_____

_____

_____

Vision / Purpose

Values, beliefs, boundaries, ethics, morals, needs, wants, and your mission are all interconnected elements that shape and guide your vision and purpose for the rest of your life. Here's how these components can be utilized:

Values: The fundamental principles and qualities that we hold dear and define who we are. They serve as the foundation for our decision-making and behavior. Identifying our core values allows us to align our vision and purpose with what truly matters to us, ensuring that our actions are in harmony with our deepest beliefs.

Beliefs: The thoughts and convictions we hold about ourselves, others, and the world around us. They shape our perceptions, attitudes, and actions. Examining our beliefs and challenging any limiting or self-defeating ones enables us to expand our potential and create a more empowering narrative for our lives.

Boundaries: The limits we set to protect our well-being, honor our values, and maintain healthy relationships. Establishing clear boundaries allows us to prioritize our needs and values while respecting the needs and boundaries of others. By setting and maintaining healthy boundaries, we create a supportive environment for pursuing our vision and purpose.

Ethics and Morals: Provide a framework for distinguishing between right and wrong, guiding our behavior and decision-making. Integrating ethical principles into our vision and purpose ensures that our actions align with our values and contribute to the greater good. It involves considering the impact of our choices on others and the world around us.

Needs and Wants: Identifying and understanding our needs and wants helps us clarify what is essential for our well-being and fulfillment.

Needs are the core elements necessary for our physical, emotional, and spiritual well-being, while wants represent our desires and aspirations. Aligning our vision and purpose with our needs and wants enables us to pursue a life that satisfies both our fundamental requirements and our deepest longings.

Personal Mission: The guiding purpose and overarching vision that gives direction and meaning to our lives. It encapsulates our values, passions, and aspirations and represents the impact we strive to create in the world. Our mission serves as a compass for setting goals, making decisions, and living authentically. It provides a sense of purpose and fulfillment as we navigate our life's journey.

By integrating these elements into our vision and purpose, we create a holistic framework that reflects our authentic selves and guides us towards a fulfilling and meaningful life. It allows us to live in alignment with our values, honor our boundaries, make ethical choices, meet our needs, pursue our wants, and make a positive impact through our mission. This integrated approach helps us cultivate a life that is purpose-driven, values-driven, and aligned with our deepest aspirations.

Vision and purpose are two interconnected concepts that provide direction and meaning to our lives. Here's a description of each:

Vision: Refers to the desired future state or the ideal outcome we envision for ourselves, our communities, or even the world. It is a compelling mental image of what we aspire to create, achieve, or contribute to. A vision serves as a guiding light, inspiring us to work towards a better future and motivating us to take action. It reflects our deepest aspirations, values, and dreams.

A vision is not limited to a specific area of life but can encompass various aspects, such as career, relationships, personal growth, or societal impact. It goes beyond immediate goals and focuses on a broader and more long-term perspective. An unobstructed vision provides clarity, focus, and a sense of purpose, guiding our choices and actions along the path towards its realization.

Author's Note: My personal vision changed when I had my breakdown. It used to be about how I could assist everyone else in achieving their goals, whether it was family, employment, or relationships. I was always trying to "fix" and "help" everyone else. That is a heavy burden for those around you, because it makes them feel that they don't measure up to your standards. And it was so disempowering to me, keeping myself out of my own alignment. I used to think that putting others before myself was a gift I was giving, now I know better.

My personal vision and the purpose of this book is to assist as many people as possible in understanding, aligning, and integrating the innate knowledge of their true self through the universal laws and the electromagnetic, biochemical world we live in, so that EVERYONE lives their best life.

Purpose: Is the underlying reason or the "why" behind what we do. It is the sense of meaning and significance we attach to our actions, endeavors, and contributions. Purpose arises from our values, passions, and strengths, and it connects us to something greater than ourselves. It's about understanding our unique gifts, interests, and talents and finding ways to use them in service of a greater purpose.

Having a clear sense of purpose brings a profound sense of fulfillment and satisfaction. It gives us a reason to wake up in the morning with enthusiasm and a sense of direction. Our purpose can manifest in various forms, such as making a positive impact on others' lives, pursuing a particular career or creative endeavor, contributing to a cause we deeply care about, or fostering meaningful relationships and connections.

Do you see how vision creates a purpose, which when aligned with values, beliefs, boundaries, your ethics, and morals become a fully integrated version of self?

Vision and purpose go hand in hand. While vision represents the destination or the desired outcome, purpose fuels the journey and provides the motivation and sense of meaning along the way. A compelling vision that aligns with your purpose can be a powerful driving force that propels you forward, even in the face of challenges and setbacks. It helps you stay focused, resilient, and dedicated to creating the impact you envision.

When you mix vision and purpose together, they provide a roadmap for our lives. Allowing us to live intentionally and authentically. They inspire us to set meaningful goals, make choices aligned with our values, and cultivate a life that reflects our true essence. By connecting our vision with our purpose, we can create a life that is not only successful but also deeply fulfilling and purposeful.

I hope you truly see the power you have when all parts of YOU are aligned with your HIGHER SELF. I hope you understand that you have the responsibility to follow your dreams and passions and not play small. It is selfish not to.

"At the center of your being you have the answer.
You know who you are and you know what you want."
—Laozi

Romanized as Lao Tzu and various other ways, was a
semi-legendary ancient Chinese Taoist philosopher,
credited with writing the Tao Te Ching. Laozi is a
Chinese honorific, generally translated as "the Old
Master", from 571BC.

CHAPTER 6

How Do You Overcome Self-Doubt and Self-Sabotage?

Stories You Tell Yourself

Someone who has given me strategies for effectively managing stress or tricky situations is Brené Brown. I encourage you to use her approach when dealing with personal beliefs, stressors, or relationships.

When something occurs, try saying, "The story I am telling myself is..."

For example, imagine you've asked your partner to take out the trash and they've agreed. However, you notice the trash remains untouched over time. Without addressing it, you begin assuming negative things about your partner. This builds up your arsenal of grievances as you observe and wait but, still, nothing changes except for the trash growing larger and emitting an unpleasant odor.

Did you know that suppressing something not only triggers stress hormones and causes inflammation, which can lead to health issues, but it's also like holding a beach ball underwater? You can only keep it submerged for so long until it inevitably shoots up, in any direction, leaving you at the mercy of the consequences.

Eventually, your suppressed anger explodes, leading to an intense argument with your partner, where both egos vie for righteousness, walls are erected, and the relationship starts crumbling.

Unless you deliberately intend to end the relationship, what value is there in such turmoil? Even then, there are better ways to handle it.

Consider using Brené Brown's approach and approaching your partner, saying, "There's something bothering me that I need to discuss. The story I am telling myself is that you haven't taken out the garbage because you don't respect me or value our relationship. These thoughts trigger painful memories, and I'm afraid our relationship might end just like my previous ones."

How do you think your partner would respond to that? Especially if they followed the same method and replied, "The story I am telling myself is that I can't believe I forgot again. I value you, and I don't want you harboring negative feelings towards me or our relationship because your opinion and respect matter to me."

What are your thoughts on this approach?

I encourage you now, to reflect on five momentous events in your life, focusing on the challenging ones. Apply this method to each event by asking yourself, "What story am I telling myself about this event? What does this event reveal about me and the overall situation?"

The deeper you delve into this exercise, the more liberated and empowered you will feel.

Use Relativity and Polarity to see Potential

Let's now look at those five major events in your life and apply the Law of Relativity and polarity to it. This is the way I work with my clients. I have them stand in the middle of the event.

For example, think back to when you were in the fifth grade and got yelled at by your teacher for not doing your homework. Take a few moments to stand in that event. Notice how it feels. Is there anything you can let go of? Any anger or resentment? How does it feel to do this?

As you move through the event, try to stay connected with your inner self and how the event made you feel. This is an important part of understanding your internal narrative and how it impacts your overall life experience.

From there, begin to look at the event from different perspectives. How does looking at it from the teacher's point of view change your understanding of what happened? Can you relate to why your teacher was so angry? Is there anything else you can learn from the experience that may be valuable for your growth? How does this version of the story make you feel? Does it empower you or disempower you?

Now turn forty-five degrees looking at that event from another different angle; how does it look? Keep looking at it from alternate versions. Maybe you were late with your homework that day, but it was because of a family crisis. Your teacher didn't know about this and so the reaction seemed unwarranted at the time. How does looking at it from this different angle change the way you feel?

Finally, turn around to the other side and look at yourself in the event. What did you learn? What did you do right in the situation? What could you have done better? How can these lessons be applied to other situations in your life? What resources or skills can you use to empower yourself more when faced with similar events in the future?

Through this lens of examining different angles of an event, we can begin understanding our internal narrative and gain deeper insight into our lives. It can help us move through difficult or challenging times, as well as provide clarity to the decisions we make in life. As we do this work, it's important to remember that things are not always black and white; there is often a spectrum of possibilities for understanding events. By looking at them from different perspectives, we can begin to form a deeper understanding of our experiences.

By engaging in this type of reflective practice, we can start making changes in our lives and create new narratives that empower us.

Remember: Your story isn't told to you by others – you are the author of your own narrative. It's up to you to decide how your life plays out.

Your internal narrative is always changing, so don't be afraid to adjust it over time as needed. There is no right or wrong answer – just go with what resonates most with you now.

Finally, look at the event from a place of appreciation. Can you find any unseen benefits in it? Is there anything valuable that you can take away from it and apply to other areas of your life that will help you continue to grow?

At this point, CHOOSE the story that is best for you today. Remember, the event is in the past. The perspective and story is now your choice. Take away what you want from the event and let the rest of it go.

Author's Note: I lost someone in my life that I thought would never leave me. This person was probably more important to me than I was to myself. The loss was so profound. I carried it like a massive weight on my back. I would tell people, "You don't understand how much pain I am in and what I have lost." After going through these exercises myself, I saw the loss as necessary for me to grow and expand. I realized I could never get to my full potential if I made someone else more important than me.

I look at it now like the transformation that a caterpillar goes through in order to become a butterfly. It was messy, hard, and necessary all at the same time. When I changed my story about that loss, it changed how I felt about myself. My feelings of accepting it, and understanding that it was necessary for me to lose that relationship, made it comforting rather than painful. It made me realize that everything happens for a reason, and there is a purpose greater than we can sometimes see in the moment.

This is the power of getting to know yourself through the lens of internal narratives. If you take the time to understand why things happen in your life, then you will be able to make more empowered decisions about how to move forward. Give yourself the space to explore and get to know your own story, and you can start creating a life that is truly your own.

The next time something happens in your life, take a moment to reflect on it using the Law of Relativity and polarity. By understanding what happened from different perspectives, you can gain insight into who you are and how best to move forward. You might even be surprised by what you learn about yourself!

In the end, it's up to you to decide how your life story will play out and what stories you will tell yourself. With a little self-reflection and internal inquiry, you can start creating an internal narrative that empowers and inspires you.

Make it what you want it to be. Make it your own.

Only you know what is best for you. Let go of what no longer serves you and move forward.

Perspective Proven by Science

Scientists were trying to figure out what really makes up tiny things inside atoms. They did a special experiment called the "Double-Slit Experiment." First, they set up the experiment to check if the center of an atom acted like waves, and guess what? It looked like waves!

Then they got curious and set up the experiment differently to see if these tiny things could also act like particles. Surprisingly, they saw particle behavior too!

This got them scratching their heads. How could something be both a wave and a particle? It sounded crazy! But then they had a lightbulb moment. They realized that the way these tiny things acted depended on what the scientists were looking for. It's like they could change their behavior based on what the scientists expected to see.

Imagine you have a toy that can turn into a car or a plane depending on how you want to play with it. These tiny things inside atoms were like that. They could be whatever the scientists expected them to be.

This was important because it showed that reality can be tricky. It's not just about what things are, but also about how we look at them. The experiment shook up our ideas about how the world works, and it's still a big topic scientists talk about today.

There are recent scientific findings that atoms can be in a "paused state." According to an article in Neuroscience Magazine, scientists are not sure how this is connected to the black holes in our universe, but they do know that black holes make up the majority of our universe.

Think of it this way: Some atoms have already been declared as a wave or particle – based on the intention of the observer which is the – *Universal Law called Observer Affect*, but most of the universe is in a state of pause. This is really exciting new information. Can you imagine what our universe can become? Can you imagine that you can create anything you want?!!!!

This connects with Dr. Bruce Lipton's discovery that our DNA and cells change based on the environment the cell finds itself in. You can take an event and you can rewrite the story any way you want, which changes the reality.

Author's Note: I personally used this on grudges I had with my parents. (There is not a person alive who doesn't carry some pain or resentment from their parents. Our brains are just wired that way).

Remembering that I carried a belief and bias that I did not matter, and our brains are set up to be right and find proof of that belief, when I looked at all the sides of an event, I realized that I could choose any point of relativity that I wanted and thereby create my own reality. I looked at all the events that caused me internal pain and used the previous exercises to examine the events with the Law of Relativity and the Law of Polarity.

In that scenario I could be the victim, I could be the hero, I could be any archetype that I chose. Which meant, I needed to ask myself, "Do I want to choose something that empowers me and pushes me forward, or do I want to choose something that disempowers me and holds me down?"

We create our identity, beliefs, vision, and purpose. Now it's your turn to choose which version of the past aligns with your chosen identity.

This is where your power is. It is in your choice and your decisions.

Begin looking at past events in your life from all relative points of view. Even look at the polar opposite of what you thought it was. All of these viewpoints exist. Which one do you choose?

That decision should be easy if you did the work from the previous chapter of discovering who you choose to be.

Healing Exercises

There are many healing exercises you can do to heal from past traumas, but it depends on where you are emotionally as to what you do here. Do you have your foundation of needs? Do you feel safe? Do you feel ready to release the demons of your past that are holding you hostage?

A professional therapist or counselor can do some healing exercises with you. Like the ones I use on my one-on-one clients, but because of the strength of the exercises and the profound effect they can have, I will not describe my methods here.

Author's Note: If you are in need of a professional and would like to be one of my one-on-one clients, please contact me using the contact information in the back of this book.

Emotional trauma can have profound effects on a person's mental, emotional, and physical well-being. It occurs when an individual experiences an overwhelming or distressing event that exceeds their ability to cope, leading to a sense of powerlessness, fear, and intense emotional distress. Following are some common effects of emotional trauma.

1. **Psychological Impact:** Emotional trauma can disrupt a person's sense of safety, stability, and trust in the world. It may result in symptoms of anxiety, depression, post-traumatic stress disorder (PTSD), and other mental health conditions. The individual may experience intrusive thoughts, flashbacks, nightmares, and emotional reactivity related to the traumatic event.

2. **Emotional Distress:** Trauma can lead to intense and long-lasting emotional reactions. The person may feel overwhelmed, fearful, irritable, or emotionally numb. They may struggle with regulating their emotions and may experience frequent mood swings, emotional outbursts, or a persistent sense of sadness and despair.

3. **Disrupted Relationships:** Trauma can impact an individual's ability to form and maintain healthy relationships. They may struggle with trust, have difficulties in establishing boundaries, or experience challenges in developing intimacy and close connections with others. Social withdrawal or isolation can also occur to protect oneself from further emotional pain.

4. **Negative Self-Perception:** Trauma can deeply impact a person's self-esteem and self-worth. They may develop negative beliefs about themselves, feeling guilt, shame, or a sense of worthlessness. These negative self-perceptions can lead to self-destructive behaviors, self-sabotage, or a constant need for validation and approval from others.

5. **Physical Health Consequences:** Emotional trauma can have physical manifestations as well. The ongoing stress response triggered by trauma can negatively impact the immune system, leading to increased vulnerability to illness and disease. It may also manifest as physical symptoms such as headaches, gastrointestinal issues, chronic pain, or sleep disturbances. Many times, cancer is even related to emotional trauma.

6. **Coping Mechanisms:** To cope with the overwhelming emotions and distress, individuals may develop unhealthy coping mechanisms such as substance abuse, self-harm, avoidance, or dissociation. These strategies provide temporary relief but can further contribute to long-term difficulties.

7. **Impact on Daily Functioning:** Emotional trauma can significantly affect a person's ability to function in their daily life. Concentration and memory may be impaired, leading to difficulties at work or school. Sleep disturbances and intrusive thoughts can disrupt daily routines and activities.

It is important to note that everyone's experience of trauma is unique, and individuals may exhibit different responses and coping strategies. Healing from emotional trauma often requires professional support, such as therapy or counseling, to process and integrate the traumatic experience, develop healthy coping mechanisms, and restore a sense of safety, self-worth, and resilience.

Emotional Healing

As a Certified Emotion and Body Code™ Practitioner my preferred method of dealing with emotional healing is with this energy modality. If you have never heard about it, let me explain it in my own personal way.

Suppressed or unprocessed emotions get trapped in our body. Those trapped emotions are chemicals and hormones that did not get processed through our lymphatic system.

This is why we dig up bones, but why should you be re-traumatized by events that you cannot change? There is an effortless way to release these holds and bad effects lingering in your body. It's with the healing energy from a certified energy healer. Because of the dramatic healing I experienced with the Emotion & Body Code™ it has naturally become my preference. That is why I use it with all my clients.

The Emotion and Body Code™ taps into your subconscious mind through energy and consent and asks the subconscious mind to lead us to the trapped emotions, so we can release them. Because this work is done energetically, I can work on my clients in person, together on video chat, or by myself with the client's consent. The results are totally transforming and never cease to amaze me.

The subconscious mind is binary and cannot describe or tell us anything, so it's up to the healer to ask the questions needed to find the suppressed emotions. In a session I can either begin with something that is on the top of your mind or something that is bothering you with pain. Or we can ask your subconscious mind what it thinks the priority is. By asking yes or no questions with the map created by Dr. Bradley Nelson, we can move through the rabbit hole of your body to find the trapped emotions and then release them energetically. They can only be released when the subconscious mind has been fully heard and all the needs met for that event, but a trained practitioner can release only about three major trapped emotions in one session.

This was the major secret as to how fast I healed my personal past, and the amazing results that I have seen with my clients. Once a trapped emotion is released, it can never come back. This alters the chemicals in your body, reduces your inflammation and then changes your DNA, so the next generations do not carry the DNA of that event.

Mind-blowing. And the way of the future. Think about it, our western medical system is based on disease. Our pharmaceutical industry is based on creating lifetime clients. They are a business and usually have shareholders that are looking for return on their investment. Their metrics are not based on healing people and then losing the client. That would be a bad business plan.

Our medical system is broken. It almost doesn't matter where you are in the world; the system is full of holes, inefficiencies, and silos. They are not addressing the root cause and the whole person.

My favorite quote from Albert Einstein is, "The medicine of the future will be frequency based."

Frequency is the rate of vibration of energy. Everything is energy. Energy cannot be created or destroyed. Why would energy healing and holistic medicine be deemed to be fraudulent or useless? Why have we been discouraged from learning about the energy of our bodies and how we have the innate power to create and heal?

Could it possibly be MONEY and GREED? Let's consider some facts:

Twenty to forty percent of most doctors' education is based on learning about pharmaceuticals and their interactions when combined with more than one drug. Even after a student graduates and receives the title of "Doctor," Big Pharma sales representatives continue educating them on the newest drugs. This part is understandable, everyone wants their doctor to be informed about the newest and most cutting-edge technology, but what isn't acceptable is that when doctors agree to use these drugs on you they are given a compensation package for using them, which equals more $$$$ in the doctor's pockets and bank account.

In the late 1800's when chiropractic medicine began it was rejected by the established medical community. Many people were wary of chiropractic's unconventional approach to healthcare, and there was a perception that chiropractors were not adequately trained or regulated. I am old enough to remember, as a young adult, chiropractors being looked down on by the medical doctors.

Dr. Christiane Northrup, a double board certified doctor who taught at one of the biggest and most prestigious medical schools, was banned from discussing that there was a connection between health and the food we ate, because it was deemed heretical.

Many of our laws are designed and created by lobbyists representing Big Business and Big Pharma. Guess what their focus is? *Hint: Not your health and wellness.* They represent corporate business so their focus is profits and return to shareholders.

Authors Note: While going through my healing period I went through and experienced many traditional medical and psychiatric methods. One of the most traumatic experiences I faced was when I met with my psychiatrist for the first time. He had me go through and list every trauma I had experienced in my life. When we were done, he handed me a list of meds to take and dismissed me. It was horrific. It was too much for me - or anyone for that matter to handle. This was one of the darkest moments in my life. And it came to me after the encounter with someone I trusted would help me.

At our next meeting I addressed it with him; he said his role was only finding the right drug combination for me, it was not working with me toward my wellness. I told him that my hair was falling out due to all the medicines he prescribed me. He then told me about another drug I could take to stop the hair loss. Can you believe that???

Did you know how the American Standard Diet was created? It was not from the medical community. The food pyramid was designed by business lobbyists, government agencies, and public health organizations. Since then, obesity, mental illness, and disease have skyrocketed. We now need labels on our food to tell us what's in it. Currently there is a large push to put stringent laws on natural supplements. Do you think they are worried that we are getting sick from vitamins?

Big Pharma, and all big business, employs the same people who told us smoking and cigarettes were perfectly healthy. They told us that Monsanto spraying our crops was within tolerable limits. They told us that GMO foods were better than what Mother Nature created. Industries were created around elevating our stress while big businesses told us the value of stress, and how good we were to be working so hard for our jobs.

Have you noticed that it seems every week there is a new report telling us what foods cause cancer, giving the news media yet another front page story? All that does is confuse people as to who and what they should trust. This is another way we are being disempowered, because then "experts" can tell us what we should eat, how we should lose the weight. More and more industries are being created around these so-called newsworthy stories. Nobody is talking about the real cause – inflammation, and how it is the cause of all disease. Inflammation is created by our immune system because it is trying to protect us from an alien substance that our body doesn't recognize. Do you think it might be all the chemicals and preservatives they use in our foods for extended profits?

I could also go on about how laws deemed childbearing as a blight against the business industry, and that it should not be seen as a natural part of life. That left women punished for bearing and raising the children, and the demands placed on men were increased. These laws separated families and were detrimental to our children's upbringing.

But, let's return to my original topic of energy and money.

Money is energy, and energy cannot stay stagnant; it must keep moving. Money flow is as abundant as air or water, because it is energy. It must keep flowing. Our birthright is abundance and being a part of the flow.

But when GREED dams up the flow it breaks universal laws, and it is unsustainable.

We are in a paradigm shift right now. I believe that all of us are RisingUP to be our best. We are creating new systems, breaking the old ones that disempower and go against universal laws. It's happening right now.

This is your time to RiseUP. I encourage you to heal your wounds and trauma using energy healing, in whatever way is best for you. I encourage you to explore the Emotion and Body Code™ and find someone to be part of your healing team.

Author's note: If you would like me as your coach and on your healing team, please do not wait to contact me. I am on a mission to bring this message and heal as many people as possible, so in the very near future I will only be training others to heal, and not working as much with one-on-one clients. If you are interested in an energy healing session with me, my contact information is at the back of this book. If you are interested in becoming a certified practitioner, I will have a QR code in the back of the book under Dr. Bradley Nelson's bio so that you can become your own energy healer.

Choose whatever works for you, but you must choose. Because now that you know there is energy healing available, you can't unknow it. That means if you get energy healing or not, you ARE making a choice and a DECISION. I encourage you to do it purposefully and informed.

"Move fast and break things. Unless you are breaking stuff, you are not moving fast enough."
—Mark Zuckerberg

American computer programmer, business magnate, internet entrepreneur and philanthropist. He is known for co-founding the social media website Facebook and its parent company Meta Platforms.

CHAPTER 7

Thriving in Transition: Navigating with Confidence and Clarity

Create Identity

Congratulations, if you did all the work in the previous chapters. I bet you feel amazing, and you're ready to take on the world. Now, take my hand and let's step into your greatness.

Get ready, because I'm sharing with you the biggest secret and the best tool you can use to create anything in your life you want . . . it's:

Your power of CHOICE and DECISION.

The biggest choice or decision that you will ever make is by answering the question, "Who are YOU?" and "Who do YOU CHOOSE TO BE?"

Never underestimate the power of identity. How you define yourself is how you live your life. The words, the language, and the energy that you produce all come from creating your identity.

The words I AM.... are the most powerful words in the world.

Since you have done all the above exercises, you are ready to make this choice. You are no longer going to be that person based on what you endured and what life threw at you. You now can choose what the meaning is for all of those events.

Now, who are YOU?

If you identify yourself as your job or your career, then who are you when you retire?

If you identify yourself as your position in your community or your family, who are you when changes happen?

One of the main reasons why many of us experience mental health issues like depression and anxiety is because we lack a clear identity of who we truly are in our own minds. But our body and spirit always know our true identity – who we really want to be.

If you get out of alignment with who you are, your body and spirit will speak up in different forms of communication. Being split from yourself or feeling lost from your true identity takes all your power away. That leads to negative feelings of hopelessness and depression.

Take time to really create and decide what your identity is based on YOU. Who are YOU? Hopefully, the previous exercises have made this the most important part of finding your inner power, inner resources, and inner highest self. Now put your identity into words in the space provided.

Claim your identity. Choosing who YOU are will feel exhilarating.

The Real Me

Emotional Vibrations

A psychiatrist named Dr. David R. Hawkins discovered the power and energy of quantum physics, and the distinct power of the energy associated with our emotions, when working with his patients. As he continued his work he created the chart of the energy of emotions. The chart below will show you what he discovered, which has been scientifically proven to be true.

You will notice that the powerful emotions are the highest vibrating emotions like peace, joy and love. That's why everyone in the world is seeking it. It's where we belong. It's our birthright. This is where we are naturally ourselves.

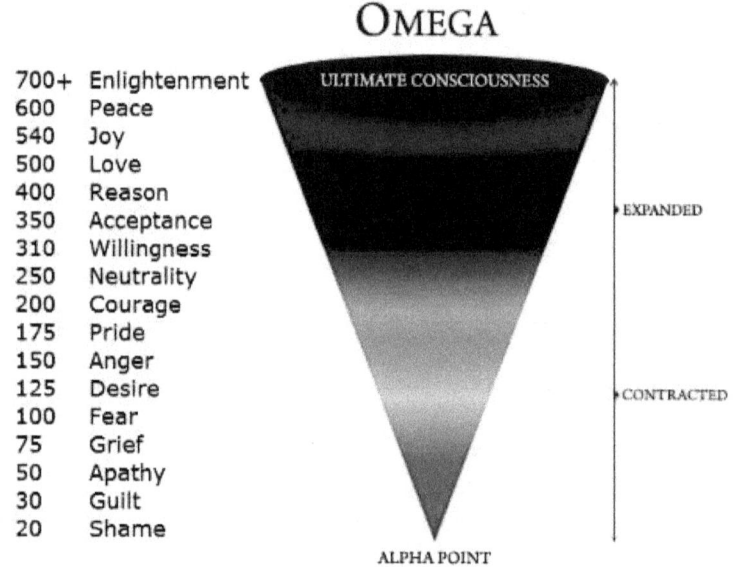

Shame is on the opposite end of the spectrum and is the lowest vibration. Shame is not a natural emotion for humans; it was imposed on us by judgment from outside of ourselves. Judgments like failing, not fitting in, or not doing what is supposed to be done. These are all external morals imposed on you by someone else's definition.

Just because someone dumped or vomited their baggage, opinions, judgements, or expectations on you does not mean you need to accept it. It is theirs. Not yours. They are probably trying to feel better by giving it away and not having to do their own work.

There is a famous story of an angry man going to see a high monk. He vomited all his anger on the monk, and when he was done the monk smiled and said, "I love you." Someone who was watching asked the monk why he didn't get angry, and why he took all that from that man when he didn't deserve it. Then the monk smiled and replied, "If someone gives you a gift and you refuse to accept it, who owns the gift?"

When you are feeling ashamed of yourself, know that you are choosing to receive an outside judgement that has been given and placed on you. It's not yours to carry. It is being imposed on you by someone outside of you. It is your choice whether you give it back to them or accept it.

Do you know that the only vibration lower than shame is death?

When we are experiencing these emotions, we are energetically vibrating and sending out energy vibrations that match where we are. That is why sometimes we feel stuck. If our intellectual brain decides on a higher emotion or higher result, and our internal emotions and beliefs are not in alignment with that vision, it's like we're playing a game of internal tug of war. We're being pulled from both sides. When we do this, one side or the other either falls in the middle mud pit or we call it a draw and neither side wins.

Remember your power is in choice and decision. Power doesn't mean easy or fast, but it is your POWER to create.

Thinking that you can shoot up the charts from guilt and shame and go straight up to love and joy is just wishful thinking. But you can carefully climb the ladder of emotions. Start slowly. If you are feeling shameful, you can change that to guilt.

Example: I am so ashamed of myself for getting into all of this debt. Well, I got myself into all this debt – I'm guilty. *Now you're ten vibrations higher than before. Keep going.* Okay, oh well – this is my life (apathy). *Now you're thirty vibrations higher than where you started.* I feel so sad that I'm in this predicament (grief). *Now you're fifty-five vibrations higher than before.* Oh, crap!!! What in the heck am I gonna do (fear)? *Now you're eighty vibrations higher than before. Keep going . . .*

You don't have to climb the ladder of emotions rung by rung; you can skip over some of them. Just take it moment by moment and choose. Your power is in your CHOICE and your DECISION. I've already said this a time or two, but I can't stress it enough because it's so true!

I know it is hard at first but it gets easier with repetition until it becomes efficient and part of your unconscious program.

Let's get back to how you raise yourself up the energy funnel. How do you eat an elephant? One bite at a time. You RiseUP your energy one step at a time.

If you are feeling guilty about something, can you get yourself to fearful? That is three large steps up.

When you are fearful can you get yourself to anger? Again, that is another two steps. From anger can you get to accept that whatever it is, just is? You cannot change it, but you can change your story about it.

From acceptance you are now rising into your power, and you can now find reason in your intellectual brain. Once you're here you start to purge the chemicals created by stress hormones and you're turning the switch of your central nervous system. Now you can begin to see clearly.

Can you see how you are truly in control? Only you hold the power. Do you see how *Unlearning the Crap* of what has been the quicksand of your environment is your key to reaching your true potential?

Stress as a Powerful Energy to be Harnessed

We've already discussed how stress is detrimental to us, physically, emotionally, and spiritually. Let me repeat that to make it clear. Unprocessed stress is detrimental to us. It's unproductive and harmful. But stress that is harnessed and processed is a powerful energy force that we need to move outside of our comfort zones.

Author's note: I like stories and analogies because that's how the brain remembers and processes information. It's important for learning and remembering. The analogy below will help you understand.

If an airplane is sitting at the hanger, parked with the engine off, there is no stress. There is no destination and no movement. The airplane is stagnant, but it contains pure potential. A choice must be made: stagnation or potential.

The choice is made that the plane will take passengers from New York City to Tokyo. The decision now has a vision and purpose; it's a fantastic start. Now the passengers also have their own vision and purpose of taking this flight.

But this is still not enough to move the plane. Even with all that focus, vision and purpose, the plane still has no energy to move. This is where many people have misunderstood the power of the Law of Attraction. They got to this step and waited.

Now let's bring in the *Law of Action*, which states that *inspired action with passionate emotions creates*. The pilots, the airlines, the entire airport staff, the passengers, the flight crew, the ground crew, must all be in unison and together in inspired action. This is when things begin to move.

The Law of Compensation tells us that we will be compensated equally for our energy and contributions and the Law of Polarity states that there is an exact opposite to everything.

That plane still does not have enough power or force to be equally compensated to get off the ground – UNLESS there is stress and resistance. For the plane to fly, it needs to gear up its engines and create enough inspired actionable force that it can be compensated equally after pushing through the resistance . . . and that push is called stress.

The most dangerous parts of a flight are the take-off and landing. That is where most of the stress is – in the breaking of vibrations. If we choose not to experience the stress, then we do not have the power to change our current vibrational state. Once the plane is in the air, it is now in its comfort zone because the stress has already been processed.

There must be stress and resistance to produce any change. Period.

Breaking out of your comfort zone is stressful, and you will come across resistance. See it as breaking through the ribbon of a race. A runner in a race is looking for the ribbon at the finish line. Once the runner breaks through the ribbon, the pain of running the race subsides. The stress has been utilized and the runner has now achieved the goal – winning the race. He or she now has the momentum of being a winner and finishing the objective. And we know the Newtonian law, an object in motion (or state, or thought, or belief, or dream or vision) *will stay in motion until it hits resistance.*

The Universal Law of Polarity states there are two sides to everything. For instance, if you want to go from one side to the other, you must create resistance and stress to get there. If you want to go east, you must leave west.

Consider the stress and resistance as proof you are on the right track and moving in the right direction, so keep going. It is NOT a sign that you are going the wrong way if you have made the decision to go there. It can only be seen as a warning sign if you are unconsciously crossing the comfort zone line.

While we are on the subject of planes, let me veer off track slightly. Do you know how a plane's autopilot works? The destination and route are plugged into the autopilot. *This is the same as you decide on your vision and purpose. These things need to be plugged deep into your subconscious mind or autopilot – your beliefs.*

When resistance kicks in taking the plane off course, the autopilot corrects it and gets it back on track. The autopilot is constantly course correcting. It knows there will be winds of resistance pushing against it, and it prepares for that. As each departure from the route carries it slightly off course, the autopilot calmly corrects itself. The autopilot has not failed when it goes slightly off course, because it knows in advance that it will happen, so it's built right into the system.

Many times, people give up and feel they have failed when hitting the resistance. This is the time instead to accept the fact that resistance is part of the journey and start course correcting.

Any negative emotions associated with going off course temporarily will be kept to a minimum, if you know that it's normal, natural, and expected. Instill a belief that says, *when resistance l happens, I have all the resources I need to get back on track; I can handle any opposition or obstacle that is in my way.*

Resistance and going off course are part of the journey. You will be pushed off your course a time or two. There will be obstacles. There will be times when you stop paying attention and find yourself facing in a different direction than you were intending. This is when you accept that it's normal and natural. Then you calmly course correct. You don't beat yourself up or tell yourself disempowering thoughts. This could coerce you into aborting the journey. But when you understand that it's part of the journey it doesn't faze you.

When we know and understand that everything is part of the biomechanical, electromagnetic energy system that follows Universal

Laws – we align our vision and purpose to work within that system, and we are in flow.

If we try doing things on our own, with force and willpower, pushing and pulling – swimming upstream, all we end up doing is staying stagnant and creating exhaustion. It is that predictable.

I do believe that faith is part of our journey, but I believe that faith comes from knowledge and understanding, not from just trusting an outside source. Your inner heart and higher self know the truth when you hear it. It resonates and they sing, "Yes, yes-yes-yes!"

When you get into that alliance, your journey has energy, attraction, rhythm, compensation, and vibrational alignment attached to it. You are now working with the natural forces instead of against them.

Why we have been trained to believe all of that is possible for machinery, industry, and business, but not for ourselves, is one of my biggest purposes and the reason for my vision. We need to Unlearn the Crap that we have been fed for centuries.

We are not separate and different from our universal world. We are not special or an exemption to the rule. We are a part of the universal law of continuous expansion. Your personal expansion is part of the universe. You are denying the power of whatever you name your God, when you disempower yourself, or when you cut yourself off from your dreams and your vision. When you disempower yourself and play small, you are saying that God made a mistake with you. Do you see how impossible that is?

Author's Note: I hope that this truth, knowledge, and understanding give you the faith you need to thrive in any transition you may choose.

Mindfulness and Living in the Moment

Now we come to some questions I know you are wondering about: "How do I stay in my power?" and "How do I keep my identity intact in a society that is trying to keep me enslaved to them?"

This is how and why you can do it:

- Energy is always moving and changing.
- Energy cannot be created or destroyed.
- Energy can be a wave or particle based on the relativity of our beliefs.

That means there is nothing but this moment, and this moment can be anything you choose it to be based on your beliefs and perceptions.

How do you do that?

Through your senses. What are your senses telling you right now? What do you feel? Is it warm or cold where you are right now? Is there a breeze or a fan blowing on your skin? What do you hear? If you listen, can you hear birds singing or horns beeping? What do you taste? What do you see? How do you feel emotionally? How does your body feel? What part of the emotional vibration chart are you at in this moment?

This is what is called mindfulness. Mindfulness is when you are consciously aware of the moment you are in. By practicing mindfulness, you are directing your energy. When you notice or feel your mind or body is not in harmony, ask yourself this question:

Is this what I want to choose?

If not, choose something else. Okay, I hear your ego mind crying, "But it's not that easy; change takes time."

That is NOT true, and here is a perfect example of why.

Let's say you're single and you choose to get married. You're standing at the altar, or wherever you choose, and you're asked if you will commit to this person in sickness and in health, for richer or poorer . . . and you make the DECISION to say YES.

Now your identity has changed in one second. You were single a second ago – now you're married.

Before you decided to say yes, your identity was that you were single or engaged. And the morals, values, and boundaries that fit that identity would be how you would behave and live.

After your DECISION your identity has changed and now you're married. It happened in the moment of DECISION. Your identity changed and that changed your values, your vision, your behavior, your choices, and your life direction.

The process of getting to your choice and decision is what can take time – if you choose it to.

Or you can also jump right to the choice and decision. Either way you are choosing.

Every single moment, every single now, you are choosing. Are you choosing by default because of your unconscious conditioned mind? Or are you making a conscious choice?

You may have endured trauma and abuse in your past. You may have gone through horrific events (fear, grief, anger). Nobody can change that. It happened. It was horrible (acceptance). The question now is, can you choose to be courageous and face the event, release the energy of the trauma, and let it go (courage, willingness).

After you choose to go through the process, you now get to choose what is next. Do you continue to RiseUP the funnel of emotions and choose to step into your power, or do you choose to give in and let it consume you?

Remember, you can only drown by the water you take in. The water left on the outside of you lets you float along the river of energy.

Do you choose hard now to have easy later, or do you choose easy now and have hard always?

And by the way, who labelled stepping into your power as hard? Who made us believe that everything should be easy and that we should not experience pain?

Our pain is our GPS telling us we are going the wrong way, or we're breaking through to the other side. If you numb yourself from your feelings to make it easy, then you cut off your connection to your inner self and the communication it is trying to give you.

Do you realize that numbing and easy are marketing ideas to sell you a product? Big business, our conformity-driven society, and 5% of the world's population who controls the money, laws and power, are banking on the fact that you will become dependent on their product to produce the feeling you want, and thereby become a lifetime client. Do you really want to give someone else your power when you can create your own feelings any time you want?

I understand that there are times when we need to not feel pain, like after a physical trauma. Sometimes we need to numb the pain in order to heal better. I understand that sometimes we are weary and need a break, and that's okay. There is a rhythm to life and we need to listen: awake - asleep, up - down ... This is the Law of Rhythm. You were never ever meant to be strong all the time.

Energy is constantly moving. Accept the fact that you go through rhythms in life. Accept that there is a Law of Timing and gestation. Putting pressure on yourself for what you "SHOULD' be doing, feeling, or experiencing is all a choice.

This can be a tough pill to swallow. It means that:

- You are responsible for your life.
- You are the creator of your experience.
- You are the master of your purpose.
- You are powerful beyond measure.
- You have been programmed to think that you have been disempowered by your weakness or fault. It is NOT true.

Accepting radical personal responsibility is stepping into your own power. Responsibility does not have to be a burden; you can choose it to be your superpower.

*"The best way to succeed is to have a specific Intent, a clear
Vision, a Plan of Action, and the ability to maintain Clarity.
Those are the four Pillars of Success.
It never fails!"*
—Dr. Steve Maraboli

Life-changing speaker, bestselling author, and Behavioral Science
academic. His empowering and insightful words have been
shared and published throughout the world in more than 25
languages. Dr. Steve has delivered his inspiring, entertaining, and
unforgettable speeches in over 30 countries, earning numerous
awards while being enthusiastically praised by the media.
His quotes and videos have become a social media sensation,
being shared by millions across the globe.

CHAPTER 8

Discover Yourself:
Hidden Dreams and Desires

Your Self-Discovery Process

It's time for the fun to begin! It's time to completely surrender your egoic, conditioned mind and really enjoy this exercise, mentioned in the previous chapter. If you promise to wholeheartedly embrace this exercise you will be totally amazed by its power.

Since I don't want you to be confined to the space available in this book, I want you to find a journal – preferably an empty one – and begin writing everything, and I mean EVERYTHING that answers the following questions. Do not censor yourself. Do not bring in the buts. Be silly and fun, be profound, be practical, be magical. Do not stop writing when you feel a pause in your thoughts. Your ego will give you resistance. You know this must happen. Accept it and allow your inner self to surface by just holding the pen on the paper. Do not lift it up. Just wait, you will be given the answers. I promise.

This is just a free flow of thoughts. Ok? Are you ready?

- I want...
- I like...
- I wish...
- I love...
- I hate/dislike...
- I don't want...
- I wish I could get rid of...

This is a tough exercise even if you just stay on the surface. I want you to go deeper. Ask more. Get more. Get crazy. Let it all out. Add to it when you think of more.

Journal

Now that you have your journal, describe how you felt about that exercise. What did it bring up in you? Use your journal every day and when you do, do not lift the pen off the book, keep moving even if you are doodling for at least 10 minutes.

There is a mind/body connection that happens when you keep the energy moving. There is an opening of old doors, and old limitations that are revealed to you. Just keep writing, keep pouring it all out, even if it doesn't make sense, because this is not a time for rational thinking. This is not the time for the intellectual mind to be in charge. This is a time for connecting to your inner, higher self, the part of you that really knows you. The part of you that you can trust. The part of you that will never harm you.

Do this exercise of journaling every day. This is how you discover yourself and open the doors that have been sealed shut inside of you. Sealing those doors was only a coping mechanism. Now it's time you free yourself.

I have a free journal prompt book that fits into this journey. The link to this resource can be found at the back of this book. I encourage you to access it, and use the prompts to really dig deep into who you are.

Personality Test

Another way you can discover yourself is by taking personality tests. The science that has been put behind these tests is amazing. It will reveal your truth if you answer the questions quickly with no thought, just automatic pilot. You will discover things that make you happy, proud and excited. It will feel really good when you can feel and see who you truly are.

Sometimes it can be a bit upsetting when we see truths that were not realized before. But the point of taking these tests is putting the truth out so we can see it clearly. Then we are able to make informed decisions and choices about how we can use our strengths. This will help us go in a direction that will expand our strengths even more, so we can be of great value to the world.

By following your innate strengths, your inner desires, and your deepest dreams, you will be living fully empowered. You will be living on purpose, with passion and peace while creating prosperity for yourself and the world.

Author's Note: I began RiseUP Coaching because I wanted to share the knowledge and experience I have accumulated over the last 40 years. Even with all of my many studies and experiences, I know that I can't be an expert in everything, so I want to share the resources that have been instrumental to me in my own personal growth and journey.

The Personality Path, found at https://personalitypath.com/free-enneagram-personality-test/?ref=11&swcfpc=1, is the most comprehensive personality assessment test I have tried . . . and I have tried many. Some were designed for employment or aptitude testing, but this one captures the essence of who you are. If you want to experience profound and in-depth knowledge of who you are naturally, visit the website above and take your own Personality Path test.

Authors note: I have been a serial entrepreneur my entire life. I am always coming up with ideas and they tend to be ahead of the curve. Unfortunately for me, I carried limiting beliefs which I have shared which created self- sabotage for all those businesses.

So I went the traditional route and got J.O.B.s I could fit in for some time, but there was always a place where my passion and zeal for constant improvement collided with my employers. When I did my personality test it was clear that it was not just a coincidence. That is the strength of my inner personality and, while I am a great employee for employers who just let me work hard, I am a really bad employee for someone who wants to micromanage me. It is just who I am. Knowing this is what gave me the courage to make the decision to leave the corporate world and create RiseUP Coaching.

Knowing that my strengths and natural passions aligned perfectly with helping others and being autonomous, it became an easy choice. Learning about yourself through personality tests like the Personality Path can really make a difference in your authentic alignment.

A Movie that Changed My Life - *The Wizard of Oz*

I encourage everyone to watch The Wizard of Oz movie. Even though it's from the 1930's, the lessons and analogies still apply today. Watch it and apply it to yourself and your life. It's entertaining and very enlightening

Here are two pivotal moments for me:

1. In the middle of the movie, Dorothy, the main character, finds herself at the mercy of the "All Powerful Wizard of Oz." She is feeling helpless. She feels like the whole world is attacking her. She knows she can find her way home and she keeps trying, but the obstacles are big and hard. She needs to find the strength to go on. After arriving at the place where she was told to go to attain the power and knowledge needed to go home, she finds only a man behind a curtain pulling levers and buttons to make it look as though he's controlling her world. The Wizard of Oz finds himself exposed and says, "Pay no attention to the man

behind the curtain," while desperately trying to regain control of Dorothy and his all-powerful image. However, once the curtain of truth was exposed, Dorothy could never again not know it. The knowledge had become inseparable from her.

2. At the end of the movie, Dorothy, who had been desperately seeking to find her way back home from a place where she didn't fit in and didn't want to stay, finally finds her way. But before leaving she looks at her mentor and guide, the good witch, who tells her, "My dear, you've always had the power, you just had to find it yourself."

"Always go with the choice that scares you the most,
because that's the one that is going to require the most from you.
Do you really want to look back on your life and see how
wonderful it could have been had you not been
afraid to live it?"
—Caroline Myss

An American author of ten books and many audio recordings about mysticism and wellness. She is most well-known for publishing Anatomy of the Spirit. She also co-published The Creation of Health with Dr C Norman Shealy MD - ex Harvard professor of neurology.

Curiosity

One of the greatest qualities we have is our curiosity. Being curious about anything and everything that catches your attention will allow your inner guide to show you more about yourself than you could ever imagine.

Have you ever walked down a street and something caught your eye? Did you stop to find out what it was and why it caught your attention? Did you ask yourself, "I wonder what this is, and I wonder if I would like it?"

I wonder..? What if I tried...? I am curious...? What does this mean?

The quality of your life is determined by the quality of your questions. Curiosity drives your questions.

Ask yourself high-quality questions and you will begin to see high quality results. What you already know has gotten you this far, in order to get more out of your life you need to learn what you don't know. Of course, this will keep you out of your comfort zone, but it will also add spark, energy, and excitement to your life.

Facing Your Fears

What scares you the most? Do you know why it scares you? Did you inherit this fear by osmosis from someone in your family, or did you have a traumatic experience? Like self-limiting beliefs, fears are also keeping you from experiencing your true potential and inner self. It's time to examine how they are affecting your life. Do they keep you safe, or are they keeping you small?

Once you examine a fear and really look at how it's affecting you, you can decide if you want to release the energy of it or keep it because of the importance for you to continue holding on to it. Once you take a good look at the fear, you will find that it has no value. It might actually be the resistance and stress needed for you to cross over to where you ultimately want to go.

Reflection of Life's Pivotal Moments, Regrets, and What Ifs

What ifs are dangerous. Dying with them is even worse. I've watched a couple of people who were very important to me die with their regrets surfacing in their last moments. Usually the what ifs are accompanied by a fear, but they can also be attached to lost moments, unfollowed dreams or desires, and making choices that are not aligned with the true you.

There is only one you, and only you can deliver the gifts you have. The experiences you bring, and how you touch people in your own special way, can only be done by you – no one else. Only you can bring you to the world by stepping into your authentic self, following your dreams, and releasing the past baggage.

Dying brings every what if to the surface. Wouldn't it be better to address your what ifs while you are living, and decide whether or not you want to follow them? When you make a decision, there are no what ifs left to regret.

Identifying Your Patterns and Themes

Take a look at your patterns, and the themes that repeat themselves in your life. It could be financial or relationships. It could be anything that repeats in your life.

Are these patterns serving you today? Do they work with the identity you have chosen? Do they align with your chosen beliefs?

Patterns and themes are beliefs and thoughts that are repeated enough in the physical world to facilitate easily identifying the root. When we have our habits and patterns aligned with our authentic identity, vision, and purpose, we can put much of our workload on autopilot. Our subconscious mind is designed to create efficiencies in our life, freeing us up so we can continue to create and evolve.

Choose wisely instead of through happenstance.

Visualization

Do you know that your subconscious mind can't tell the difference between what is real and what is imagined? Your thoughts are real energy, and your thoughts are things. Imagination and visualization can create reality for your unconscious mind.

Almost every athletic, professional, or personal success has an element of visualization to it. Think of everything that you have wanted and planned for: vacations, holidays, projects, even everyday dinner. They all have an element of visualization to them in order to be created.

Your consciousness is one of the greatest tools you have to create anything you want. Everything, and I mean everything, requires consciousness to be created. That has been proven by quantum physics. What the scientists don't know and probably never will is the consciousness behind our original creation.

Putting your consciousness and focus on anything, imagining how it will feel, what it will look like, and how it will change your life, really does create your reality.

The opposite is true as well. Worry is negative visualization. Thoughts become things and, if you are thinking worrying thoughts and visualizing worst case scenarios, you are in effect creating the very things you do not want.

Your brain can't tell the difference between actual physical reality and what is imagined. It also can't comprehend a negative. When we think of negative things, saying we don't want them, the very fact that we are putting our visualization, our focus, and our attention on it makes our mind, frequency, and our attraction to it align with its very vibration.

One of my pet peeves is the *Don't Drink and Drive* campaigns. Our brain does not know the word "don't" so what gets repeated over and over again is *Drink and Drive*. What if we used words like Drive Sober? Isn't that a better alternative?

The Power of Language

"Sticks and stones may break my bones, but words will never hurt me." Seriously???

Who made that crap up?

Maybe it was a do-gooder who obviously didn't understand the power of creation. Or maybe it was just another way to disempower us by altering our beliefs. Words have thought, emotion, and pure energy behind them. Once that energy goes out in the world, it can never be destroyed.

The Oxford Dictionary says the definition of an ion is: an atom or molecule with net electric charge due to the loss or gain of one or more electrons.

Ions are electrically charged energy. It means energy in motion. The root of this word, "mot" comes from the Latin which means to move with energy.

Let's look at some more words, and what their origins actually mean:

Passion:

Origin: From the Latin word "Passio"

Meaning: what sustains you while you suffer

I am so passionate about my work. (I am suffering for work.)

Addiction:

Origin: From the Latin word "Addictus"

Meaning: betray, abandon, sell out, devote, sacrifice

I am addicted to this relationship. (I have sold myself out and betrayed myself for this relationship.)

Motivation:

Origin: From the Latin word "Motivus"

Meaning: moving cause

I just don't have the motivation to go to the gym. (I do not have a cause to create the necessary energy.)

Justification:

Origin: From the Latin word "Justificare"

Meaning: to make right

The CEO's passion for growth was his justification for implementing risky business practices. (The CEO suffered to make things right when they were high risk.)

Emotion:

Origin: From the Latin word "Emovere"

Meaning: move

My emotions are out of control. I wish I could shut them down so I can be normal. (My ability to move with energy is out of my control; I want to stop being moved with energy.)

Inspiration:

Origin: From the Latin word "Inspiratus"

Meaning: breathe into

I woke up this morning with the inspiration to clean my closets. (The energy was breathed into me to clean my closet.)

Decision:

Origin: From the Latin word "Decidere"

Meaning: to cut off

I keep making the decision to go to the gym but I never actually end up going. (I have cut off the energy of other options, so I will go to the gym. If not, I will cut off the energy of going to the gym and explore other options.)

Determination:

Origin: "determinare" (to set limits, decide)

Meaning: The quality of being resolute and unwavering in pursuing a goal or making a decision.

I am determined to reach my goals this year. (I have decided to set limits and boundaries around my time, and I use all my energy on this decision. It is final. No other option exists.)

Creation:

Origin: From the Latin word "Creare"

Meaning: to bring forth

I have a deep desire to create something meaningful in my life. (I want to bring forth my gifts with energy.)

Education:

Origin: "educare" (to bring up, rear, educate)

Meaning: The idea of guiding, nurturing, and developing a person's growth and potential. It involves leading someone, especially a child, out of ignorance or immaturity toward greater knowledge, skills, and maturity.

Our education system is based on learning marketable skills for a job.(Our education system is not guiding and developing the person's individual potential, which is why self-education and development are so important now.)

Sensation:

Origin: "sentire" (to feel, perceive)

Meaning: The process of experiencing physical or emotional feelings through the senses.

Her voice had a calming sensation that eased the tension in the room. (Her voice vibrations touched my skin, I then felt the vibrations of tensions leave the room. This told my central nervous system it was safe to relax.)

Celebration:

Origin: "celebrare" (to frequent, honor, celebrate)

Meaning: An event or activity held in honor or appreciation of a person, place, or significant occasion.

I believe it is important to celebrate my wins. (I honor my wins, showing myself that I honor and appreciate my efforts.)

Depression:

Origin: "deprimere" (to press down)

Meaning: A mental health condition characterized by persistent feelings of sadness, hopelessness, and lack of interest or pleasure.

She was in a deep depression. (She was physically, mentally and emotionally pressed down and didn't feel like she could get herself up.)

Isolation:

Origin: "isolaris" (to make into an island)

Meaning: The state of being separated or detached from others, often physically or socially.

When I am depressed I tend to isolate myself. (When I am pressed down and can't get myself up, I detach myself from anyone who could help me get up, which leaves me stuck.)

Corruption:

Origin: "corruptio" (to spoil, ruin)

Meaning: The act of dishonestly or improperly using one's position or power for personal gain or to damage something's integrity.

Our social systems have been corrupted. (Our society has been spoiled and ruined by the dishonesty and improper use of power and it is no longer sustainable.)

Innovation:

Origin: "innovatio" (renewal, change)

Meaning: The introduction of new ideas, methods, or technologies that lead to significant improvements or advancements.

The educational system is in need of innovation to adapt to the changing needs of students. (Our system of guiding and finding the individual's potential is in need of change and renewal to provide the true needs of a student's potential.)

Words are powerful. They are the language of our vibrations. Listen to the words you use, both verbally and inside your own mind. Know that the ones inside your mind are the MOST powerful because you can't escape them. You can choose to keep or reject any word in your thoughts by catching a word that doesn't serve you, and changing it into one that does.

Thoughts take only about sixteen seconds to strengthen and continue. I want you to imagine that your thoughts are like products on a conveyor belt. Every automation system has a built-in quality control element to it. It has a laser eye that sees the products that don't meet the standards, and with a fast flick it is gone.

Imagine how much simpler life would be if you could think of your thoughts in this conveyor belt manner. Immediately tossing the ones that don't meet your standards. It's time to stop identifying with the thoughts that don't serve you. Reject them – flick them off of the conveyor of your life. And by all means never attach yourself to the thoughts that don't suit your higher self.

It could go something like this: (Try hearing a mechanical sound when you do this – just for fun.)

Thought #1 - Good.
Thought #2 - Great.
Thought #3 - Interesting, I never thought of that one before.
Thought #4 - NOPE . . .REJECT!
Thought #5 - Good . . .

If there is no charge or energy behind a thought within that time period, it will just move on. But if you take that thought and ruminate over it, or feel controlled by your thoughts, then you strengthen that very thought into existence. Do not fool yourself by thinking words do not matter.

Here's an equation for you to memorize for the rest of your life:

Thoughts + Words + Visualization = POWERFUL ENERGY

Personal Strengths

We all have strengths and weaknesses. I prefer saying that we all have natural aptitudes and can't be everything at once. While we may be able to swim, it is not the same natural ability that a fish or dolphin has. It is important to understand and appreciate your natural tendencies and strengths. They will lead you to your inner calling.

If something in your life is not a natural strength, either don't do it or find a way to delegate it. When we try to force ourselves to go against our natural strengths it would be like that dolphin trying to learn to walk. It is a lot of wasted energy for nothing. The dolphin's life is not improved or expanded by working hard to learn to live like land animals.

If you find that you naturally are drawn to the arts and numbers overwhelm you, then the best solution is to find someone that loves numbers for your personal finances. Hire an accountant or bookkeeper. There is no value in you diluting your time and talents by investing energy into that which is not authentically you.

Nature

Spending time in nature, in quiet solitude, is one of the best ways to connect with yourself. The energy and vibration from Mother Nature is powerful. Allowing yourself to align with it helps you RiseUP to the vibration of pure consciousness and creation. Nature naturally raises you up.

There is a process called grounding that I use on a daily basis. We were not born into a world of shoes, concrete, and buildings. Our homes used to be shelters in caves or in other natural settings. The electromagnetic energy that you connect with when you are in physical contact with nature has more healing capacity than you may have acknowledged. There is no profit in discarding the buildings, clothing, and shoes that prevent us from experiencing the benefits of touching, feeling and connecting to nature.

Have you ever noticed that great ideas come to you in the shower? The negative ions in the flowing water actually calm down the positive charges of stress in our busy lives. I will repeat, we are electromagnetic beings living in an electromagnetic field.

Spirituality & Inner Guidance

Removing outside noises allows your inner voice to be heard. When in solitude you can more easily connect to your intuition and your heart. Your body's communication, and guidance system, need to be heard in order for you to step fully into your authentic self and power.

We all have our own personal preferences when it comes to religion. Every religion is based on certain values and beliefs that have purpose. I respect your belief in whatever religion you practice, but there is a distinct difference between spirituality and religion.

The point I am making is this: we all have an inner spirit. It is pure energy. It is pure consciousness. It is pure love.

The Universal Law of Energy states that energy can't be created or destroyed. It can only be transformed or transmuted.

Your inner spirit, your inner energy, your inner guidance is connected to all other energy in this universe. There is no place where energy does not connect and exist. Your spirituality, your heart, your soul, and your exquisite essence are precious gifts.

Spirituality involves genuinely establishing a connection with your true self. It's about engaging with your inner spirit, which is intricately linked to everyone and everything.

There are many avenues that you can choose to quiet your mind and connect with your higher self. Find what works for you to become intimately connected to the real you.

CHAPTER 9

Creating Vibrational Harmony: Embracing the Magic of Synchronization

Start with The End

Over 20 years ago I met Raymond Aaron for the first time at a convention. I was immediately sold on his mentorship program on how to create a life vision. He had me go through my epitaph and my eulogy. What did I want to be said about me at the end of my life? If I could write my own eulogy of my accomplishments, the difference that I made in others' lives, and who I was, what would I say?

Let me tell you, it's not an easy exercise imagining that far into the future. Trying to really understand that we get to choose the impact we want to make in this world. I don't remember how I answered it twenty years ago, but obviously I got off track. However, it never left my mind. When I sat down to write out my identity, beliefs, vision, and purpose years later, I realized how right he was then, and how right he still is today.

Every moment matters. Every encounter, every action, everybody matters. That is what entanglement is about. Once someone comes in contact with another, there can be no separation from it. It always stays with you as part of who you are.

Vision for who we are is only part of the creative process of designing ourselves. We now need to create a vision for our life. How will we live, where will we go, who will we impact, how will we be of service to others?

Take some time and think seriously about how you want to be remembered: what you stood for, and what difference your life made to others and the world. Remember that you are made of pure potential, and so is every single moment of your life.

If you can envision it, you can then bring in the Law of Inspired Action, invoking the Law of Correspondence and Attraction thereby rising and utilizing the Law of Vibration and Resonance. All of the Laws of the Universe are completely connected. You can't use one without the other.

Remembering that every obstacle has the seed of opportunity built into it, then applying the Law of Polarity and Law of Relativity, you stay on track with your dreams. The timing of your vision is within the Law of Rhythm and Gestation. Never give up. Never give in because it must happen – by law – if you stay with the energy and focus.

Now that you know you truly have the power of creation at your disposal, what is the vision of your life going to be?

Practicing Visualization

Since you are doing your part of following inspired action and learning the lessons along the way of your breadcrumb trail, now it is time to visualize.

Your subconscious mind cannot think or create. All it can do is accept what it is given and create efficiencies with it. Knowing how your brain works makes it easier for you to visualize your dreams. See them in color and in detail.

The most important part of visualization is your emotions. They are your fuel. Use your emotions purposefully for the execution of your dreams. Every athlete who achieves greatness knows the visualization process. Feeling it over and over again changes our brain and trains it for future experiences. Visualizing creates the pathways that become habits. And your habits become your reality.

Make these five sentences your mantra for life. They will help you stay focused in every moment:

- Watch your thoughts, for they become words.
- Watch your words, for they become actions.
- Watch your actions, for they become habits.
- Watch your habits, for they become your character.
- Watch your character, for it becomes your destiny.

The Law of Compensation says you must be compensated for your energy and contributions. This is why knowing how to rewire your brain through techniques like visualization, repetition, and emotional choice is crucial to getting what you want in life. But there are three more steps that are needed to make it all come together and they are: selecting your own personal and true identity *(being the person who you really want to be)*, visualizing your dreams and desires every day, and then following through with action from the inspiration you are receiving.

Once your dreams are decided upon and you've taken the first step, you must trust that it will come. The Law of Gestation or Timing states that everything has a time and process that must happen before it is created. We have no idea how long the manifestation of our dreams or goals will take. Under all circumstances remain hopeful. Knowing that when the opposite shows up, it doesn't mean you failed. It means turn around and choose again. Remember, you will attract everything on the same vibrational frequency as you.

Author's Note: Here I am almost at the end of writing this book and as I write this sentence it occurred to me that writing this book is an example of how this worked for me. Writing has always been a passion of mine. When I was a struggling teenager, poetry writing healed my heart.

When I was a young adult looking to find my inner strength, powerful business writing always produced results for me. During my dark difficult times, I would journal constantly; and now I journal for self-discovery, not just healing.

People had told me my whole life that I should write a book but it didn't seem realistic for me. I think I told you that my old life was about serving others, not myself. Somehow, somewhere, a book was inspired into me about everything that I had learned my entire life. I saw it and I felt it and I will admit the first few pages were intimidating.

After I completed the outline, I made the decision to continue writing. I saw and felt it all in my heart and mind. Then synchronicities came into play, people arrived, resources, everything just fell into place without my efforts. And somewhere along the way I realized that I have never felt more alive and more me than I do writing this.

My heart is pounding, my nerves are all on alert. I know this is the sign that I am exiting another one of my own comfort zones. Knowing that these bodily sensations are communications from my inside, I choose to make these feelings excitement and not fear. I am choosing my labels and my meanings of what I am experiencing.

Do I know what will come out of it once I have created it? No, but I consider it just like giving birth. When I sent my children out into the world, once they were on their own, they were no longer mine. And I know soon I will have to surrender this process and send it out into the world, and let it be what it will be. But I have to say the writing of vibrational frequency and experiencing it at the same time really is so empowering.

What do you have inside of you that you didn't allow yourself to dream or believe in? Where has your life's journey taken you that will lead you to where you are meant to be? We do not know the ending of our life when we begin, because we are always creating ourselves. Join me, and do it purposefully with intention and let the rest of the world deal with their stuff. After all, you haven't come this far with me to not jump into your own authenticity.

This is what is meant in The Law of Correspondence, when it states that what is outside is inside. If you are not liking what you are experiencing on the outside - your experiences - then you need to go inside and change it from there.

> *"To be yourself in a world that is constantly trying to make you something else is the greatest accomplishment."*
> —Ralph Waldo Emerson

American essayist, lecturer, philosopher, abolitionist, and poet. He led the transcendentalist movement of the mid-19th century. He was seen as a champion of individualism and actually went by his middle name Waldo. He was a prescient critic of the countervailing pressures of society.

Entrainment

Before I share my favorite resources for easily and effortlessly rewiring your own brain, let me share a phenomenon that exemplifies how the universal laws work. Entrainment is the process of synchronization. It was discovered centuries ago when a clockmaker was designing clocks that stayed in the correct time for sailors who sailed across the oceans. At that time, sailors needed to use the stars and time to determine their position to guide them. Having a clock that kept accurate time was extremely important to them.

The clockmaker noticed that when he set each clock's pendulum at night, they were all tick-tocking at different timings. When he woke in the morning every clock was synchronized. After repeating this over and over again with different scenarios he realized that each clock's sound vibrations synchronized them together.

Entrainment happens everywhere in our lives because we are all energy and we are vibrating. The Heartmath Institute has proven that heart rates can synchronize between people who are heart to heart.

Do you know when babies are born, they are immediately placed on their mother's heart to connect their signals and bond them together? Their hearts synchronize, but let's take that a little further. Walk with me on this one. We know that birth is traumatic for both the mother and the child. The baby has now entered a world that is totally different than the one they just left. Talk about leaving your comfort zone. The synchronization of the mother's and child's heart beats must tell the baby that they are still safe. We know that the heartbeat slows down when the parasympathetic nervous system kicks in after stress. We know we are biochemical beings, so hormones such as oxytocin are released for both, which creates bonding. Everything in our lives that we need has already been born into us. We came into this world with an internal guidance system that works biochemically, electromagnetically, and energetically. Does this give you a strong sense of foundation like it does me? I hope so. You don't need to figure things out, you just need to choose from all that is available.

Author's Note: My father had retired to another country and he was passing away. I had known for a long time he was sick and I thought I had come to terms with his passing. When I went into the ICU for the first time, I was shocked. Death was written all over him. I could see his energy being sucked out of him. When I left the ICU I broke down and sobbed. A woman came to me and held me tight, and whispered in my ear words I did not understand, until I heard the word for Jesus and realized that she was praying. She would not let me go until my heart rate connected with hers and I calmed down. Then she let me go and I never saw her again. Talk about everything being shown to me at that moment. Energy, love, connection, vibration, gestation. All of it. I had many magical pivotal moments during that time of my life but this one was so profound for me.

One of my clients told me a story of what happened when her father was in the hospital with atrialfibulation – this is when your heart goes out of its normal rhythm. He was having quite a time and things weren't looking good. As soon as my client and her mother walked into the hospital room where her father was staying, his heart immediately went back into its proper rhythm.

Like our heartbeats, synchronized breathing happens in group activities like singing, yoga, and breathwork healing. If you ever have the chance to go to a breathwork group run by a certified practitioner, you will experience the power of not only your breath helping to heal, but the synchronization of the entire group and room becomes one powerful vibration, raising the healing to everyone in the room.

I was blessed to be a part of a Jaitara Jayde breathwork event that healed the sexual trauma I was carrying from being abused in my past. Jaitara is not only a certified breath practitioner, but she has other certifications that make her an expert in healing past sexual trauma. I would highly recommend her if you have trauma from your past that you are ready to let go of. You can find her resource information in the back of this book, along with many other resources I am recommending. Please, tell her Kathy sent you and make her day.

Women's menstrual cycles often become synchronized when they live together. This is not only because of the entrainment of vibration but also because of the hormones that attract each other. This is another example of living in a biological energetic world, and how it rules everything.

Another fascinating story about entrainment comes from a documentary I watched, about buildings and how they defied our expectations. Some engineers built a bridge and there was a big opening ceremony where thousands of people gathered to walk across it. As they began walking, the bridge began swinging and swaying. It scared everyone half to death. For over two years the bridge was shut down while the engineers tried to figure out what went wrong. They finally realized that the pedestrians began walking in synchronization. The combined energy and vibrations were transferred to the bridge. Through this story you can visually see how the power of synchronized vibrations works.

The documentary also gave another example of how British soldiers were ordered to walk out of unison when crossing bridges because in the past bridges had collapsed when they walked across all in sync.

We have been raised in a world that says if I can't see it then it doesn't exist. What we don't see is the majority of our universe and its power. With your newly found knowledge you can utilize that power consciously and intentionally to create your desired outcomes.

Brainwave entrainment is my favorite because it is very personal to me. It has allowed me to not only heal, but to break the ties of self-limiting beliefs from the disempowering stories of my past. It has also helped me to focus intently on creating my future with purpose.

After using the healing methods of Neuroptimal that helped me so much, I also became a certified Neuroptimal Neurofeedback Practitioner. This is not something where I can share or recommend a particular practitioner because it must be done in person. It is an amazing way to heal and clean up past programming in your brain by allowing it to identify what is not in your best interest and clear it away.

It is done by connecting your brain through EKG electrodes and then showing the brain the patterns in the brain waves that are happening. Your subconscious mind is always trying to do the best for you, but it needs the effect of the Law of Relativity in order to see itself. This system gives your subconscious mind the feedback it needs to see which programs are working for you and which are not. With repetitive sessions, your brain can heal itself, thereby making room for you to perform at your best.

Rewiring Your Brain

By this time in the book you know how powerful the subconscious mind is. I have discussed and showed you the physics and biology of your brain being wired by the repetition of neural pathways. You've also been shown that your thoughts create your emotions which in turn create your outcomes.

Would you like to know the easy way to do all of this? In life there is always an easy way and a hard way. The easy way is to follow someone who has already learned and mastered what you want to do and learn. You do not need to be an expert in everything. Sometimes it's best not to rely on your own innate strength alone. You can borrow strength and expertise from others that have already learned the skills and gone through the experiences that are needed for you to get where you want to go.

> *"Rich people choose to get paid based on results. Poor people choose to get paid based on time."*
> —T. Harv Eker

I have been studying for over forty years. And that includes NeuroPhysics, biology, psychology, quantum physics and so much more, but in no way did I ever want to be an expert in each of those categories. I am a big picture person, not the detailed person that I would need to be, in order to be an expert in all of these subjects. I see how pieces of pictures can fall together, or what is possible. That is my SuperPower and I have learned to utilize it to its full potential and use other people's SuperPowers to fill in the gaps.

Many people in the highest positions of business, government, etc. usually don't specialize in any certain area. They have an overall concept or goal, but they rely on the individual expertise of other people when it comes to all of those minute details to carry out their plans. For the most part they're generalists.

When a Chicago paper published a series of articles after World War I, claiming that Henry Ford was an "ignorant pacifist," Mr. Ford objected to the statements and brought a libel suit against the paper. Then he made another really bold move. He put himself on the stand to prove he was not the ignorant pacifist they claimed him to be.

The lawyers hammered Ford with questions, ranging from "Who was Benedict Arnold?" to "How many soldiers the British sent to America to stop the Rebellion of 1776?" Ford didn't know many of the answers, but he was clever and replied, "I do not know the exact number of soldiers the British sent over, but I have heard that it was a considerably larger number than ever went back."

The questioning started feeling like harassment to Ford so he put an end to it when he said, "If I should really WANT to answer the foolish question you have just asked, or any of the other questions you have been asking me, let me remind you that I have a row of electric push-buttons on my desk, and by pushing the right button, I can summon to my aid men who can answer ANY question I desire to ask concerning the business to which I am devoting most of my efforts. Now, will you kindly tell me, WHY I should clutter up my mind with general knowledge, for the purpose of being able to answer questions, when I have men around me who can supply any knowledge I require?"

Who could argue with that?

You may be a specialist in one thing, but you cannot be a specialist in everything, so it is imperative that you have specialists around you in all the other areas of your life. If you are a generalist, then you definitely need a team around you, supporting your vision and helping you to succeed.

That's why I have chosen to study from many different experts throughout my life; none of them individually were able to put the pieces together because they only knew their part intimately.

We were designed to be interconnected and as a community, supporting each other, which in turn supports ourselves. When we believe we must know it all by ourselves, we are accepting the disempowering beliefs that have been instilled in us.

It is not true. It is not possible.

Here are some of my secrets: *(Not so secret, as I can't hold back and I tell everyone. And now I'm even sharing my secrets with the entire world in this book.)*

Hopefully you truly embrace the Universal Laws I've shared with you so the below will make sense to you.

Dr. Paul Scheele has been my mentor and guide for more years than I can remember. His voice is literally in my head every single day. He is the founder and creator of a technology called Paraliminals, which are available at his company, *Learning Strategies*.

What are Paraliminals?

It is nothing like you have ever experienced before. They are audios that utilize the latest brain entrainment technology. They work with whole brain learning and create deep rewiring of your brain. I choose the topic that is my intention for the day and begin every day listening to one. They take about 20 minutes, and create deep meditative relaxation and brain rewiring. You are basically choosing to program yourself and your brain to be what you want it to be.

Imagine, every day choosing your intention and enjoying a profoundly deep meditation by doing nothing more than putting on your headphones and listening for 20 minutes.

I used to carry around a package of his CDs so I could listen to them on my CD player. Then I could access them online from my account or download them to any device, but now times are moving forward faster and faster and *Learning Strategies* has now made rewiring your brain so much easier. They have an app called *MindTrx* that includes their entire library of Paraliminals along with teachings, sharing, and so much more. It is an absolute no-brainer must-have if you are serious about changing your life. And it only costs $99 a year. Imagine, you can change your life for $99.

Visit my website to and click on my affiliate link so you can get started on the life of your dreams as soon as possible. Get an app on your phone and effortlessly rewire and reprogram your brain and your life as YOU CHOSE.

Maybe you are a visual person. If this is the case, you understand that utilizing all of your senses would give you more benefits and make it easier for you to begin rewiring yourself.

MindMovies is my preference for that.

You can choose between pre-done *MindMovies* or you can create your own personalized one. It is literally a movie for your mind. If you want to visualize, but you are struggling to get your mind there, you can create your own movie of the life you want. *MindMovies* puts your ideas into a literal movie for you to watch every day for a few minutes a day. This helps you utilize the power of visualization at hyper speed.

MindMovies has been helping millions of people over twenty years and they are the experts. You do not need to take your time to become an expert in visualizing and using willpower to get your mind where you want it to go. Use the knowledge you have gained and use it to your benefit.

Visit my website to access my affiliate account for you to get your own *MindMovie* for yourself.

You have learned that everything vibrates and has a frequency. Our brain wave states are different because of the speed of the frequency.

Every thought, emotion and action is vibrating. In order to utilize the Law of Attraction, you must be vibrating in synchronization with what you desire. Then you are in alignment and resonance with your desired outcomes.

One more secret before we close this chapter. It's about the 532hz frequencies and how you can connect to that frequency easily by using the power of *Manifestation Magic* listening materials. *Manifestation Magic* uses this frequency to relax your brain, causing it to release neurotransmitters like dopamine and serotonin in order for you to feel good. This raises your frequency along with entrainment.

Visit my website and click on my affiliate link so you can experience the power of this amazing technology anywhere you are. It has become most known for its night time sleep sounds that not only rewire and reprogram your brain, but also give you deep, restful healing sleep. And who doesn't need that nowadays?

I have many more resources because I never stop learning and investigating, but the ones above are my favorites for getting you started on the path to your dreams.

CHAPTER 10

Create Your Support System

"Success comes when people act together;
failure tends to happen alone."
—Deepak Chopra

Creating Your Tribe

We were never meant to go this path alone. We've already laid down that groundwork in the beginning of this book when big business and the almighty dollar took loved ones away and our society was purposefully changed.

Nobody can achieve their own personal greatness without a support system, a community, a mastermind group... whatever it is that feels right for you, but you MUST create your tribe or your team.

When choosing your tribe, be careful. The energy of emotions gets heavier and more sluggish the lower it is on the emotional funnel. If your support system has people vibrating at a lower level than you, their pull is strong. Just like gravity – it will naturally pull you down.

Your support system must be on a higher vibration than you, so they can pull you up when you need it. If your support system has stronger and higher vibrations than you, you will naturally be pulled up and then you can RiseUP. Remember the strongest vibrations win.

You don't need to worry that your lower vibrations will reduce those vibrating higher than you because I guarantee you, they have their own tribe and team supporting them to grow as well.

I can't stress enough how important it is to make wise choices when choosing the people on your support system. Choose people who are on the same path as you, and people who have done the things you're striving for. Choose people who have already walked on the path. They are the ones who can warn you about the bumps in the road. They can say, "Don't worry I already checked this path out. It's safe. and it works. Follow me." If you want proof, science has proven that you become like and live like the average of the five most influential people in your life.

Remember: Your power is choice – choose well.

There will be people vibrating lower than you. They may be your loved ones and family. That's ok. Each of them is on their own path and travelling on their own journey of life. Let them. Let them live their lives and if and when their path brings them to a place that they are ready to RiseUP then they will be seeking their own personal support system. Soon you may be vibrating closer together than ever before.

I wonder if we were meant to be bonded forever to our birth families. Much of the animal species leave their tribe and create a new one. This is probably our biochemical world making sure that the genes are well mixed. It is a wonderful thing to have close and strong family ties, but it can also be a wonderful thing to strike out on your own.

Does it mean that there is something wrong with you if you're different from your brothers, sisters, or even your own children? When you are labelled the "black sheep of the family" does that just mean that you are different from them? If you were to see a flock of white sheep grazing happily in a pasture and happened to notice a black one in the mix, wouldn't you think that the black sheep was simply different from the rest?

I grew up with a STRONG belief instilled in me that family comes first. Family could hurt you and you had to let it go because they were family.

The guilt I felt while growing up when I wasn't aligned with some of the members of my family was terrible. I realize now, that was an outside source imposed on me. It was not mine to keep so I let it go.

Letting it go has allowed me to surrender my grown children to live their own lives as they please. I do not put requirements on what they are supposed to do, especially when it comes to me. I learned that one the hard way. My children were my gift to the world. I have set them free to be their own part of the universe. I have my own personal feelings, and beliefs from my past and I am still growing in this area, but I am aware – and I am choosing.

Remember, trying to save someone by trying to get them to live the way you think they should live and desperately wanting to help them isn't necessarily helping them. Spending all of your time and energy for others impedes and interrupts their unique path. It reduces them emotionally, and your energy can actually be detrimental to them. Let them be. Let them live their own life, even if you don't like it, or don't agree. That is ok. We are all in different vibrations and we all have different destinations. Sometimes, a kind word of wisdom or a heartfelt conversation can aid a person on their unique journey – but it is for the other person to decide if they will take your advice or not.

When you are giving all of your thoughts, time, and energy to someone else – who may or may not want it – you are purposefully taking yourself out of your power. When giving any kind of a gift you can't actually force anyone to accept it. You can't force anyone to do anything. Your gift to them is to RiseUP, and Unlearn the Crap you have been fed throughout the decades. By doing this you'll create a pathway of inspiration for others to follow.

Your brain was created for survival, not thriving. That means it will find everything that could be a danger and work hard to keep you safe. Now you know and understand why when one of those programs comes out and tries to keep you safe, you don't have to let it. You can choose to say, "No thank you." Then let it go.

Author's Note: I am feeling extremely emotional right now. This is the last chapter of this book, and I am feeling the transition. I notice that my throat tightens, and tears come down my face. I know that it is a trigger of the many goodbyes and endings I have had in my life. I honor my feelings and let them process, knowing full well that I chose this journey to get to this point. That is the difference intentional choice and decision makes. It keeps you grounded.

How will you know if it's one of those programs? Your emotions and that voice inside you will give reasons, excuses, and stories that will try making you believe you need to return to the safety of your comfort zone. This is where everything is predictable because it has already happened, and so there has been a program put in place for your future experience.

You are creating your new you. You are always in creation mode, creating a new life. This part of you does not live in the past. It resides in the future. The you that you are creating does not live in your comfort zone.

When you feel fear, that is a warning sign that you are stepping out of your comfort zone. Fear is warning you that you are on the precarious edge of the cliff and could fall. "Do you really want to be here?" it asks. then it says, "This is a warning sign! Step back! Step back!" If you are braced to a hang glider or have a parachute, your subconscious conditioned mind does not know that you have purposely chosen this, and that's why it signals you with fear.

Then you make the choice to go on ahead and power through your fear.

So you . . . Jump!

You ... Fly!

And you ... Soar!

After powering through, do you know what happens to your subconscious mind and your comfort zone? They say, "Hey, that worked. We were safe. Let's expand the comfort zone and add this program to our programming system."

And you grow. You thrive. Step by step you become the person your inner self is encouraging you to be.

Why You Need a Coach

In case you're like some of my previous clients and still don't really know what self-help/empowerment coaches do, or why you need them, let me explain.

Like the funnel of emotions you learned about earlier, there is also a funnel of personal growth. As you work your way up through each level and make it to the next one, the only way to continue to grow is to give. Coaches live to give. We give our hearts. We share our knowledge. We encourage. We elevate.

We do it because we know how vital it is to the growth of our world, and how important it is that we each do our part in raising the vibration of the world. So let's all RiseUP.

If we get GREEDY and stop the flow of energy, we become out of alignment with ourselves. The flow of energy must keep moving. It is the law. That's why coaches almost always have coaches. The energy must keep flowing in an upward expansion.

A coach can see more for you than you can see for yourself. That's because your brain is limited to what it can imagine. When a coach sees your potential, and believes in your dreams and your destination, they will move heaven and earth to support you. And this gets you there faster, easier, and in a much more enjoyable way than trying to do it alone.

You now know all the secrets of how your inner empowerment works and where it is found. You also know that your personal success is in your hands. You can no longer or ever again blame someone else for your failure. Because you and you alone have the power to create your life, and that power comes from CHOICE and DECISION.

Even though you have all of this new knowledge that will change your life, you still need a coach. All of the most talented athletes in the world know that having a coach for their particular sport is vital. The coach can see from a distinct perspective; they can see what you don't. If you find a coach that has walked the walk and knows the way you want to go, follow their lead. You don't have to hack your path through the jungle of life alone. Yes, it's possible to succeed on your own, but do you really want to take the hardest route possible? We were not designed that way. You would be fighting against universal laws by choosing that road.

Understanding the power of knowledge, purposefully choosing, and making decisions is a game changer. But it is also extremely important for you to create a support system that will help you RiseUP and not pull you down. Remember the old saying, "Your friends are like an elevator – they can take you up or down."

Find the coach that fits with you and your dreams. Find the coach that will get you where you want to go. And then pay whatever the dream is going to cost you to get you there. Payment comes through money, energy, effort, and commitment. Pay it. It will give back to you the highest returns possible if you do it gratefully. There is no greater investment than the investment in yourself.

You are that important.

Your talents, gifts and love are needed desperately in this world. Do not be selfish by withholding the uniqueness of you from the world. You are a purposeful part of this complicated system.

For many people money is a trigger. When I say pay what you need to pay some people get fearful. Because it's not actually tangible when we invest in empowerment, they fear that by making an investment in themselves they will only be losing their money. Sometimes they fear the motivations of those taking the money. They may even give them labels of greedy or selfish.

The truth is humans are wired to only value things that they have paid for. It's a known fact that if something is given to us on a silver platter it won't mean as much as if we ourselves contributed something toward it. That, my friends, is The Law of Compensation. This is where The Law of Cause and Effect and The Law of Correspondence also come into play.

You will be compensated equally for the energy and contribution you put in. For humans to RiseUP we need to step out of our comfort zone and pay the price of levelling up. What level are you seeking to reach?

Define the level of your dreams, of your goals, of your purpose, and the contribution you want to make, and then put a price on that. I think we all agree that your dreams are priceless.

I have genuinely enjoyed this amazing journey with you. As I write this I am thinking of YOU. I am thinking of the remarkable things my contribution and energy, through writing this book, will be attributed to. I am surrendering to the rhythm and timing of the universe. I am surrendering to who will be attracted to me and my vibration.

You have come so far with me. If you resonate with my style, my passion, and my energy, I have mentoring and coaching programs available for you upon request. Reach out to me by any of the means listed at the end of this book, and we will have an amazing conversation.

Remember:

- The HOW appears once the CHOICE and DECISION have been made.
- The HOW is not for you to figure out. The how is not your power.
- The WHEN is not for you to figure out. The when is not your power.
- The CHOICE . . . now that's your power!
- The DECISION . . . yes, that's your power!
- MATCHING your EMOTIONAL FREQUENCY to your DREAMS . . . you got it, that's your power!
- FOLLOW your INSPIRED ACTION with LOVE AND JOY!!!

I know, like I know, like I know – the true purpose of creation is connecting your heart, mind, and soul. It is being in full alignment and integrity with your dreams. And it's arranging your life with those dreams so that you're vibrating on their same frequency.

I'm already feeling thankful, grateful, and blessed if by chance or choice our paths cross, and I have the joy and honor of continuing in your journey.

We come now to the end of this book, which is only the beginning. You've read this book, soaked up all of its information, and you have done the base framework. You and I are now vibrating closer to each other than ever before, and I am here for you.

Take my hand, I've got you.

With all my love,

*"Surround yourself only with people
who are going to take you higher."*
—Oprah Winfrey

An American talk show host, television producer, actress, author, and media proprietor. She is best known for her talk show, *The Oprah Winfrey* Show, broadcast from Chicago, which ran in national syndication for 25 years, from 1986 to 2001

My Teachers, Mentors and Guides

Resources that I Shared in this Book

Jaitara Jayde, from the moment I saw you as a Goddess leading a large group of people through traumatic healings and releases, I saw the glow of radiant energy around you. At first I was intimidated by your strength and power, but I know that was just because I was in a healing place and you were the healer. You have been my guide and mentor through my darkness. I know that you are here to heal the dark energy of our world with your light. Anyone would be blessed to have you as one of their guides and mentors. I hope anyone dealing with deep trauma reaches out to you so they can be blessed with your healing and let that pain go. I love you. Thank you. https://jaitara.com

Grace Cirocco, my Goddess Mother, how can I ever thank you for all you have done for me. You were my mentor for so many years taking me from broken to blessed. You were a part of many of my pivotal moments, and your love and caring will always be with me. Your retreats, your groups, your personal one on one have forever changed me for the better. I love you. I thank the universe from the bottom of my heart for bringing you to me. https://gracecirocco.com

T. Harv Eker, I never personally met you but you had a profound impact on me and my life. Your Millionaire Mind weekends were so impactful for me. From there, you brought your amazing camps, retreats and other mentors. You brought a whole new world to me and showed me my own self. Every time I see someone in transition, I always recommend your Millionaire Mind weekends or your book. Thank you.

181

I wish I could have timed our connection earlier as MOSHOG is still on my bucket list. https://www.harveker.com/

Paule Scheele, I had the honor of meeting you after years of your voice in my head, guiding me. You are just as fantastic in person as you are on your Paraliminals. I can't thank you enough for bringing your expertise to the world, helping to heal wounds, and helping the world RiseUP. You are one of the Universe's purposeful creations. Thank you. https://www.learningstrategies.com/Home.asp

Courtney Smith, your contribution to my life will forever go on, just as you made such a difference in millions of people's lives. I can hear you laughing and saying we need to create pool time. May you enjoy your pool time forever. You taught me that the connection of money and our inner power is connected to being independent financially. Thank you.

Brené Brown, you are like the big sister to the world. Thank you for leading the way with vulnerability as a strength and not a weakness like the world has been trying to convince us of. Even though I did not have the honor of being personally coached by you, you coached me through all of your work, all of your books, Podcasts, and TED Talks that are life changing for everyone. The world became better when you brought you gifts to the world. Thank you. https://brenebrown.com/

James Arthur Ray, you were one of my first mentors and you opened my eyes to see the possibilities in the world. You showed me where I was stuck and how to get out of it. I have been blessed by your contributions, your insight and your strength to overcome adversity and turn it into an opportunity. Thank you. https://jamesray.com/

Dr. Daniel Amen, your research and bringing the power of the brain to my world, opened my eyes to inner knowledge that I did not know I had access to. You taught me the physical connections of neurobiology and how so much of our mental health issues are the result of the imbalance of our biochemicals. I highly recommend all of your resources to anyone suffering from any mental health issues. You are proof that we can heal ourselves when you know the facts. Your work has been instrumental in my growth. Thank you. https://danielamenmd.com/

Dr. Bruce Lipton, of all the researchers that have opened my eyes to the truth I shared in this book, the most life changing is you. You were an inspiration when I heard you speak through Hay House weekends. You proved to me and the world that we can change ourselves, physically, emotionally, financially, spiritually and any other way when we know the biochemical electromagnetic complex systems that we are. Your contributions to my growth and this book cannot be appreciated enough. We can change ourselves by changing our thoughts. We are in control of our own life and destiny. We change our DNA and those for the next generations when we take responsibility for our own healing and thoughts. Thank you. https://www.brucelipton.com/

Dr. Wayne Dyer, I can still see your face with that fantastic hat and hear your voice with your hands moving in circles as you spoke. You brought psychology into the physical world and showed me that we are all experts in our own selves. You have been and still are a major contribution to my journey. I know you were an angel to the world and I know you are happy and at peace even while you are missed. Thank you. https://www.drwaynedyer.com/

Dr. Christiane Northrup, you will have no idea how instrumental you were to my connection of the biochemical, electromagnetic energetic beings that we are. You explained the hormones and how they interact with our behavior and choices. You showed me the magic of the human body system and your contribution to my journey and this book are so appreciated. You showed me the dark side of our healthcare system and how we need to take our health into our own hands. Thank you. https://www.drnorthrup.com/

Dr. David R. Hawkins, you came into my life after you had left us. Your books brought so much clarity to me and how we are truly empowered. You connected the dots of the vibration of our emotions and how we can truly be empowered with the knowledge of emotional vibrational frequency and using that power intentionally. You are a major contributor to this book and my journey. Thank you. https://veritaspub.com/

Dr. Laura Bullard, my quantum physics mentor. I have always been trying to teach myself quantum physics. I remember when I was in my 20's going to the bookstore and buying a large book on the topic. But whoever the reader of that book was supposed to be, it wasn't me. It was too technical. When you first came into my journey, you explained quantum physics in such a way that it was accessible and understandable and available to all of us. Your teaching brought my understanding of interconnectedness of all of us and to my understanding of the world. Your teaching was the final connection that brought my understanding of everything I shared in this book together. I am still immersed in your teaching through your Quantum Transformational Teachings and I highly recommend anyone who wants to understand how I learned this, to learn from you as well. Thank you. https://theresabullard.com/

> *"Everybody has a calling. And your real job in life is to figure out as soon as possible what that is, who you were meant to be, and to begin to honor that in the best way possible for yourself."*
> —Oprah Winfrey

My Personal Thanks

While I have just shared those who I purposefully brought into my self-education and hopefully not only highlighted their individual talents, but also hopefully showed where and how I learned everything I just shared. I would be remiss if I forgot to mention the people that changed me and taught me so much just by being in my life. I need to also acknowledge their impact and my appreciation to them.

Mom and Dad, you are gone from this world, but you are not gone from my life. I feel you with me every day and I connect with you. We journeyed together; evolving together. I have taken every lesson, good, bad, and ugly of our time together and chosen what serves me and let go of the rest. You taught me that I do not need to be a perfect parent in society's rules. Every lesson was part of the fabric of my life. You are my heroes. I love and miss you both so much.

My son James. You changed me forever when you came into my life. You not only literally changed who I am but also my identity. I went from Kathy to Mom and now from Mom to Nana. All of the hardships and struggles we went through made both of us who we are and I have to say that I could not possibly be prouder of you. I am so glad that I was able to gift you to the world. I want to publicly share one of my favorite lessons you gave me. When you were a child and you were giving me a birthday present, so proud you walked up to me and said "Happy to You." When you were corrected to say Happy Birthday you looked at the person with such an incredulous look and said, "Yes, Happy to

You." Now I always wish Happy to people and my son, Happy to You. I love you. And to the readers of this I wish Happy to You as well.

My daughter Kristen. I worked hard to bring you into this world. While I thought I was creating you, I realized that I was just part of the cycle. I knew it from the moment you were born. You are your own creation and watching you evolve and stand on your own two feet and forge this world makes me so proud. I am going to share one of my favorite memories of you with the world. When you were a toddler and you tried something new, you would say, "That wasn't so easy" with your arms up and smiling proud of your accomplishments. While you can say out of the mouths of babes, I realize that sentence is so profound and has become one of my own life lessons. I love you.

Chris, our lessons of change together were profound and forever altered who I am. It wasn't easy and it is still hard. I am so grateful for the time we spent together and the happy memories I keep close to my heart. I love you.

Andre, we grew together up, out, and forward. We healed generational wounds and were there for each other. It was only for a season, but that does not change the power it gave me. Only you and I will ever know how profound our journey was, but I was blessed to be a part of it with you. Thank you.

Michelle and Melissa, I hope one day you will know the effect you had on my personal evolution. It was not easy but somehow, we worked through the fires, and we came out better on the other side. I consider myself blessed that you have touched my life and heart. I love you.

Laura, you have been one of the great gifts that the universe has given me. I see myself so clearly through your eyes and I am so grateful for what you share with me. You are proof positive of vibrational alignment. The fact that you have been such an important part of my journey made all of this possible. Thank you.

Everyone else that has touched my life, you are still entangled with me and I with you. We have become better through all of our interactions, and I am grateful for all. The song that is singing in my head right now as I type this is: To all the girls I've loved before.

To you, the reader of this. I wrote this book with you in mind. I was speaking directly to you. I hope you know that once our energies are connected, we are together for a purpose and a reason. Whatever role I play in your evolution and story, I want you to know that you have a huge cheerleader in me. I want you to succeed and lead the way with your gifts. I truly want the absolute best for you.

You deserve it and so does the universe deserve all of YOU. I hope you FLY.

About the Author

Kathy Baldwin is a multi-passionate thought leader whose own healing journey led her to develop a new paradigm for personal empowerment. Kathy is distilling her groundbreaking teachings into the book Unlearn the Crap - About Personal Success and Empowerment.

In this revolutionary work, Kathy explains how we can unlock our power by understanding the biochemical electromagnetic connections between our bodies, minds, and the world. By aligning with Universal Laws, we can break free of limitations, transcend suffering, and manifest abundant, purpose-filled lives. Kathy interweaves her intimate personal experiences with expert insights to provide readers with the keys to unlearning disempowering beliefs, cultivating self-worth, and embracing their authentic selves.

For anyone seeking to step fully into their potential, Kathy's profound wisdom offers a blueprint for transformation. This is a book about empowerment in its truest sense – the journey to our deepest power source that lies within.

Kathy's path to empowerment began during a period of depression and disconnection, when her outward success left her feeling empty inside. Though she had achieved career milestones, she found herself crumbling internally, overwhelmed by feelings of hopelessness. This spurred an intense journey of self-discovery, during which Kathy tuned into the wisdom of her body and realigned with Universal Laws. Through this process, she discovered an innate power source within herself.

By surrendering to her shadow self and exploring the root causes of her suffering, Kathy gained profound clarity about her divine connection. She learned to trust her intuition, release limiting beliefs, and live fully in each moment. Her courageous personal transformation fueled a passion to guide others to unleash their own limitless potential.

In *Unlearn the Crap*, Kathy bravely shares intimate details of her recovery, from hitting rock bottom to awakening to her true self. She provides a relatable and aspirational roadmap for readers, proving that the power to heal lies within. By distilling decades of struggle into an inspiring narrative, Kathy's raw vulnerability makes this journey both personal and universal.

Her story is a testament to the human capacity for resilience, redemption, and growth.

Kathy Baldwin has years of experience as a personal empowerment coach, helping individuals overcome limiting beliefs and unlock their full potential. She is the founder of RiseUP Coaching and her hands-on experience guiding people through transformational personal growth informs the practical, actionable strategies she shares in *Unlearn the Crap*. She provides a roadmap for readers to develop emotional resilience, reduce stress, embrace self-love and self-acceptance. Her professional experience equips her with the knowledge and qualifications to empower others.

At the core of Kathy's book is the revolutionary concept that we each have an innate ability to achieve our goals and live a fulfilling life. This power stems from understanding and utilizing the biochemical, electromagnetic connections between our bodies, minds, and the world around us.

Kathy explains how our thoughts, emotions, and beliefs create real biological reactions and energy fields. By becoming aware of these connections, we can begin consciously directing our energy to manifest the lives we desire. She reveals how our energy systems allow us to tap into the infinite potential of Universal Laws.

The book guides readers through proven techniques to align with Universal Laws that empowers individuals to break free from disempowering paradigms and societal limitations. Kathy provides actionable strategies to develop self- confidence, overcome self-doubt, and unlock one's unique talents.

Ultimately, the book enables readers to unleash their authentic potential and create abundant, purpose-filled lives. Kathy's insights offer a life-changing opportunity for self-discovery and empowerment.

How to Work with Kathy

If you are ready to Unlearn Your Crap, I am here to help you. You do not need to go this alone. How does my process work?

I have built a process that allows you to quickly identify the crap in your way. With self awareness comes the power to choose. Healing is done with different modalities and all of them can be self administered or with a guide and mentor. My programs are designed to create immediate and lasting results. Once a trauma is released, it is gone. The healing takes the repetition of implementation to Unlearn the Crap.

I only work with clients that I am aligned with and that I know I can be of service to. I encourage you to book a call with me and let's discuss your particular situation. If I am right for you, we will find a solution that works for you.

If I am not right for you, I guarantee you that you will walk away with clarity that you can use.

Check out my website at https://kathybaldwin.me and my links at https://kathybaldwin.me/links There you will find my calendar link to book a call as well as free resources.

I encourage you to read Unlearn the Crap & Level UP Your Soul is Calling. There are the details of how to do the work involved.

I would love to have you as a subscriber to my Unlearn the Crap TV show on both FENIX TV and my YouTube Channel. This is where I have discussions with people about how to Unlearn the Crap and resources that are available for you.

I do have an Unlearn the Crap Community where we are a collection of collaborators sharing our resources and asking for what we need.

I am also a founding Managing Partner for She Wins, a division of She Rises Studios, a networking group of women entrepreneurs, business owners and professionals. My chapter is located in Canada and there are other chapters worldwide. I would love for you to join my chapter and join my online meetings, even if you can't attend the local ones (all locations are open to members) There we share resources, training, offers, networking and connection. The goal is that every woman builds a sustainable, profitable business in communities that encourage thriving.

www.ingramcontent.com/pod-product-compliance
Lightning Source LLC
Chambersburg PA
CBHW071736120626
46550CB00002B/541